25 Lessons I've Learned
about ~~photography~~...Life

Books by Lorenzo

A Letter to A Muse

Art Matters

Be Yourself

StreetWise: How to be a Great Photographer,
Lessons Learned on the Streets of New York City

the lost man chronicles: book 1, the art of living

the lost man chronicles: book 2, the art of loving

25
Lessons
I've Learned
about ~~photography~~

Life

Lorenzo

New York

First printed photo edition published in the USA by Blurb.com, March 22, 2008. Second printed photo edition (with 25 new photos) published October 23, 2008. 1st paperback edition (text only) published December 18, 2008

Printed edition in B&W
Title ID: 3555533
ISBN-13: 978-1456572013
ISBN-10: 1456572016

Printed edition in color
Title ID: 3555958
ISBN-13: 978-1456574482
ISBN-10: 1456574485

Amazon Kindle edition
ASIN: B00318D6Y0 (text only)
ASIN: B004AYD6I0 (text and photos)

Google eBook edition
GGKEY: HEJBP11Y8ES

For Enzo & Dominic

Do you know what?

"You Love Me."

Yes, I love you.

I knew you were going to say that…

When you were born, you cried
and the world rejoiced;
live your life so that when you die,
the world cries and you rejoice.
Cherokee Saying

Table of Contents

Preface

Table of Illustrations

Preface

In the spring of 2005 my wife and I agreed to separate. It must have been a sign of some significance because for once we agreed on something. We had gone through years of discord, until finally, she asked me to move out.

It was either this or a divorce, and I wasn't ready to accept the latter. But I had nowhere to go. For the first few days I called all the hostels and cheap hotels I could find in New York City, but to no avail. It would just be too expensive to stay anywhere; there was a mortgage and lots of bills to pay. And since my wife stayed at home with our two children and worked part-time on the weekends, we were, for all intensive purposes, a one-income household.

In other words, we couldn't afford for me to move out.

Instead, she agreed to let me sleep in the basement of our family home, until I found somewhere to go. It was an uncomfortable alternative, but at least I wasn't homeless.

Out of shame and a stubborn streak of independence, I did not tell anyone that we were separated. Neither family nor friends were aware of my situation. As days passed into weeks, I started to feel more and more alone. I decided that I would seek help and talk to someone, someone who might be understanding and non-judgmental, forgiving perhaps; someone who might ultimately point me in the right direction.

Having grown up Catholic, one of my first thoughts was to go see a priest. They were good, guiding, and spiritually redeeming counselors.

So, on one cool spring morning, I walked into a little sanctuary called the Church of the Transfiguration, which was three blocks from my office, and took a seat in one of the back pews to listen to the presiding priest give a sermon. I had passed the church every day on my way to work for the last six years and had long felt the urge to attend one of their spring lunchtime concerts; but I always found myself eating lunch at my desk instead.

The church itself had been around for over 150 years, and for most of its history had served as a refuge for those in need. Its basement served as a safe haven for runaway slaves escaping via the Underground Railway. And during the Civil War, the founder of the church, Dr. George Hendric Houghton, took in African-Americans threatened by enraged immigrants participating in the Draft Riots of 1863, despite warnings from the police that they could not ensure his safety.

In 1870, a gentleman by the name of Joseph Jefferson sought a sanctuary to hold the funeral of his dear friend George Holland, a thespian. Rejected everywhere, Jefferson was near despair when he was led to the Church of the Transfiguration around the corner. Jefferson then responded by exclaiming, "God Bless the Little Church Around the Corner!"

The sobriquet has stuck for the last 137 years. And ever since, the theater community has frequently viewed the church as their own. In 1923, an actor's guild was formed at the Little Church, and the partnership between those of the cloth and those of the stage eventually succeeded in turning the church into an historical landmark in 1973.

In this serene place, listening to the priest finish up his sermon, I distilled my emotions and let them spill out. By the time I had a chance to speak with him, I was all choked up and had to excuse myself a few times. I could barely say what I had rehearsed repeatedly while waiting.

In those few moments — that seemed like an hour — I demurely made a request for a meeting. He asked that I return at noon.

Seven minutes before noon: I get up from my desk and walk up the block and around the corner. I enter in by the red iron gate, through the small garden, past a spray of pink blossoms, and into the quiet church office where the receptionist asked me to wait in a little room for Father Harry.

When he came in a few minutes later, Father Harry smiled and kindly asked me how he might be of service. I began sheepishly, but soon a deluge of sorrow poured out, and I broke down and wept, just like a man who had been thrown out of his home and had kept it all inside for weeks. Father Harry listened attentively. At one point, he placed his hand atop mine, and I immediately felt a certain peace, perhaps the comfort of God, overcome me.

It didn't matter that I had renounced my faith more than 20 years earlier, as a student at a college prep run by the Jesuit Order. I did, however, continue to believe in some part of what I had been taught through Sunday mass and my saintly mother; I believed strongly in the Christian principles of love, forgiveness, altruism, tolerance, and acceptance, especially in the purest sense as they were originally laid out as allegories in the Gospels that recounted important moments in the ministry of Jesus of Nazareth.

After telling Father Harry about my idea of finding a shelter or social service center where I might be able to volunteer, in exchange for a little space on a floor to sleep on and a small hook to hang my suit, he paused and then said, "We actually need a little help here ourselves. And we have an empty apartment where you might be able to stay."

At that moment I couldn't help but feel a bubbling of renewed faith. Father Harry's act of kindness reconnected me to that important spirituality, one that I had nurtured for so long as an easy-going college student in California, but that I had progressively lost hold of over the years.

For I could see in Father Harry's eyes that he believed in me, without any doubt in his heart. That moment made an everlasting impression upon me, one that inspired me to continue looking forward toward making the best of my situation.

Keeping to his promise, Father Harry informed me two weeks later that the Little Church, indeed, had a place for me to stay if I was willing to help around the house (of God). We agreed that I could occupy the studio apartment right above the sacristy, the small room where the sacred ritual vessels and vestments are stored and where the priests get dressed and prepare for mass.

The tacit agreement was that I could stay at least until June, when the apartment would be razed to make way for Sky House, a 55 story residential tower with luxury condominiums starting at $1,000,000.

Thus, I found myself living in a little church in the middle of Manhattan, in virtual isolation, for three months. During that tumultuous time, I had a chance to reexamine my life. I expected to catch up on all those books I had been meaning to read, to go to the gym, to meditate on what had happened in my marriage.

What I didn't expect was that I would end up going out every night into the city to take photos, tapping into a well of pent-up creative passion that would change my life. I never expected that viewing the world anew through the lens of the camera would prove to be an incredible journey, reminding me of some important lessons, lessons that I had forgotten somewhere along the way.

Ironically, I had given up on traditional film photography long ago, when, during my first trip to New York City in 1989, I ruined the first 35mm I ever bought by accidentally placing my oily lunch in the same tote bag. Thank God the digital revolution came along to reignite my passion, because my rediscovery of photography helped me to rediscover life itself.

Lesson 1: Everything is Beautiful

Everything has its beauty,
but not everyone sees it.
Confucius

Soon after Father Harry passed on the good news, I moved back into New York City. Although I had worked in Manhattan since I moved here from California 14 years ago to attend graduate school, I had spent the past four years in New Jersey.

What a blur those past years had been: Graduating from graduate school, taking a job, getting married, moving from Manhattan to Brooklyn; and then, when the little ground floor apartment in a brownstone became too small for a couple, their two-year old and a newborn—moving to Jersey.

Over the years I had felt increasingly trapped, as if I were going through the motions, and that my life had come full-circle to the frustrating boundaries of my youth. I was back in dreadful suburbia again, but this time with a wife, two kids, a corporate job and a mortgage in tow.

But now that I was suddenly "free," so to speak, I suddenly had to determine what I was going to do with all this extra time.

At first, I thought I would hole up like a monk and study everything that I hadn't had the time to focus on—foreign languages, art, science, philosophy, many of my greatest intellectual interests that I had neglected over the years.

Then serendipity struck. Around the same time that I moved into the Little Church, I discovered a photography website called flickr.com, which allows users to connect to other photographers around the world to share their work, their words, advice, and inspiration. I found myself eager to make such connections with others, especially since using images was an obvious way to overcome the limits of language; a photo was certainly worth a thousand words, unspoken.

One night I decided to experiment. I went out with my camera and began taking photos of the city. I was instantly mesmerized by all the vibrant colors, all the people scurrying off

1

to meet other people, and the taxis speedily transporting them from here to there.

That night the city changed before my very eyes. When I had first moved to the city, I had been awestruck by this metropolis of possibility. But once I started working, the grit, the grime and the grind of New York had quickly lost its charm, and the paranoid, frantic and chagrined attitude of the city and her inhabitants no longer inspired me as it had done before.

But suddenly, with camera in hand, the city was no longer a dark and foreboding place; it was no longer the labyrinth of a rat race. No, now, through the camera's lens, I realized how welcoming the city actually is. The camera, I discovered, allowed me to stop and look, to step out of my hurried "I've got to get to work!" or "I've got to get home" mode; the camera allowed me to focus on life itself. For the pictures see what we do not see, if only because we are too busy to see them.

Eventually, I began waiting on street corners and in the middle of sidewalks just to see what happened, to watch and appreciate the beauty of the moment in motion, and, hopefully, to get a few good pictures in the process.

At the end of the night I had taken a few hundred photos. I proceeded to edit and post these new photos online. I concluded that I would be wasting a golden, perhaps once in a lifetime, opportunity if all I did was stay inside and read every night. Besides, the books weren't going anywhere, but life was passing me by faster than ever before, and I had a rare opportunity to visually capture many of its wonderfully fleeting moments.

And on top if it all, I had fallen in love with New York City all over again.

Now that I was spending a lot more time away from my children, I realized how beautiful, how truly meaningful, they made my life. I did my best to convey this to my sons when I called them every night.

More than ever before, my boys became my favorite models. Photographing them at every chance I got, I learned and practiced the vibrant subtleties of portraiture, including the need to create and manipulate an organic environment in which your subjects will not only behave naturally, but will also evoke expressions worth capturing.

Taking up photography allowed me to embrace the present, so that I could set out to make the most of every moment, stretching each night into a lifetime, seizing every second as if to capture and tame time itself.

The 19th century poet John Keats once said, "If something is not beautiful, it is probably not true." That's because Everything is Beautiful, if only because truth itself is relative.

Hence, we must constantly remind ourselves that Everything is Beautiful; and sometimes you just have to see it from a different angle, point of view or perspective, in order to appreciate its true aesthetic worth and ineffable value.

It truly amazes me how some of the most extraordinary photos are taken of the most commonplace things, places and people—those subjects that we all tend to overlook.

All of us know of people for whom the sky is always falling or who whine about every little inconvenience, perceived insult or inconsideration. Their world is not very beautiful because they have chosen to view the world as such.

The way you choose to see the world — and life — is ultimately how the world and life will be for you. I've chosen and continue to choose to see it as something that is amazing and beautiful.

Thus, for me the truth is that we live in a world that is rife with beauty, for life itself is beautiful, and living is a beautiful thing—if only because living itself is a luxury. By choosing to see things as such, I prime myself to be open to them, to see, feel and hear them as they unfold before me.

Taking pictures allowed me to be free again, allowed me to be me again, and let me express the beauty that I saw everywhere, and in everyone.

If something is not beautiful, it is probably not true.
John Keats

Lesson 2: Everywhere You Go...

The walls were bare when I moved into the little apartment at the Little Church.

Although I had a splendid view of the Empire State Building from one of the windows, the barren walls made me feel somewhat lonely. So I decided to put up some photos I had taken in order to make it feel homier.

At the time, I was taking primarily black and white stills because I was far from schooled in how to capture motion, a moment, or simply the true vibrancy of color itself.

The wonderful thing about beginning with black and white photos is that it allows one to focus on one important element in a photo—form. Desaturated of color, a photo will reveal what I see as its skeleton: the lines, the curves, the patterns, the strong and exquisitely subtle blocks of light that together create the form of the photo.

One day, I came across a little used bookstore on 18th Street, somewhere on the periphery of Chelsea. Outside, on the sidewalk, in the clearance rack, I found a ragged old book of paintings entitled Images de la Peinture Française Contemporaine (Images of French Contemporary Painting), which I purchased for $1. For me, that dollar went a long way, for the inspiration that I derived from it was priceless. Inside the book, along with biographies of painters such as Paul Cezanne, Paul Gauguin, Pablo Picasso, Henri Rousseau, Georges Braque, and Georges Seurat, were photos of one example of their work.

After perusing through my new treasure, I got an idea. I immediately visualized how these colorful pictures could serve as the perfect complement to my own photographs.

Thus, after mounting my selections to foamcore, I interspersed them throughout the room; a colorful painting here, a black and white photo there...The paintings I chose to include were: Le Sacre-Coeur (The Sacred Heart) by Odilon Redon, Femme Qui Tire Son Bas (Woman Drawing Up Her Stocking) by Henri de Toulouse-Latrec, Les Tournesols (The Sunflowers) by Vincent Van Gogh, Odalisque by Henri Matisse, and La Sainte Face (The Holy Face) by Georges Rouault.

Besides serving as colorful decorations to the room, the work of these great painters served to inspire me, for I realized that — despite the depressing side of the separation—something special was happening to me. I was going through my own metamorphosis closeted up in this little room, this chrysalis. I was experiencing a transfiguration that would change my life forever—I was becoming an artist, something that I had wanted to be for as long as I could remember.

Looking around, I saw that the paintings I chose included pictures of flowers, Jesus Christ and harlots. I wasn't trying to be irreverent by placing these images side by side; if anything, my intentions were quite the opposite. For I strongly felt that the Christian principle of Agape—that one should love one and all—was akin to finding beauty in everything.

The Reverend Dr. Martin Luther King, Jr. once described Agape in the following manner:

> Agape is an overflowing love which seeks nothing in return, it is the love of God operating in the human heart. On this level of love, man can love his enemies while yet hating their actions. 'It is a love in which the individual seeks not his own good, but the good of his neighbor.'

Like Agape, my passion for photography became an "overflowing love" that, at first, sought nothing in return. I simply took hundreds, and then thousands, of photos because I loved doing so. It was only when blog after blog began citing my work that I realized this new avocation could become something more than just another fleeting hobby.

In addition to stirring a proactive love of beauty, art, and life, the paintings I hung up in my little room also encouraged me to pursue learning how to best use color in my photos.

I consider myself first and foremost a writer. Writing was my first love and my mistress, my whore and my confidant, as well as my muse. As a result, I take photographs as if I were writing, composing a poem about what I am seeing at the moment that I stoop or run or brace myself and then—click!

I soon discovered that every once in a while, if I was ready and equipped, I was able to capture absolutely exquisite moments when all the elements simply fell together and created a photo that was a marvel to look at.

My pursuit of this type of picture was quite akin to the art of a well known photographer and painter by the name of Henri Cartier-Bresson, a Frenchman whose style eventually came to be known as one that captures "The Decisive Moment," a term coined by Cardinal von Retz. The American publisher of Cartier-Bresson's first English edition of his work, Dick Simon, used von Retz's phrase as the title of Cartier-Bresson's book (originally titled Images à la Sauvette), the first photodocumentary of decades of his work.

French poet Yves Bonnefoy aptly summarizes the magical quality of Bresson's style in his description of his photograph Place de l'Europe in the Rain (1932): "How was he able to recognize the analogy between the man running across the plaza and the poster in the background so quickly, how could he compose a scene out of so many fleeting moments—a scene that is as perfect in detail as it is mysterious in its totality?"

Over the year following my stay at the Little Church I found that I too had a knack for capturing such decisive moments, especially as they occurred in the streets of New York City.

In retrospect, I also came to find out that Cartier-Bresson and I shared the same philosophy in regards to the equipment we used. The vast majority of his photos were taken with a Leica 35mm rangefinder camera with a 50mm lens, which in a sense is equivalent to the point-and-shoot I have used for all my photos, considering the much more powerful equipment that was available to both of us.

> In photography, the smallest thing can be a great subject.
> The little human detail can become a leitmotif.
> **Henri Cartier-Bresson**

Although I have been encouraged by fellow photographers to upgrade to something like an "SLR" (single-lens reflex), I realized that these heavier, more conspicuous, much more expensive and higher-quality cameras were not suited to my off-the-cuff, hit-and-run, street style. Cartier-Bresson believed much the same thing as he felt that he needed to carry a minimal amount of equipment because it needed to serve him as a "sketchbook, an instrument of intuition and spontaneity, the master of the instant which, in visual terms, questions and decides simultaneously."

With the aid of digital equipment though, I have been able to take this a step further by capturing a series of sequential "decisive moments," in which I have documented a moment in time, much as someone might do with a video camera, but in a fashion that stops time, so that one can actually see how a moment evolves or tumbles or explodes with action, energy, and color.

Oddly enough, a lot of people don't see this and complain that they don't understand why I post so many photos of the same thing.

"The same thing?" I often retort, if only to myself. To me, almost every photo has something new to offer that wasn't in the previous or following shot—an emerging smile, a coincidental pairing of background and foreground elements, a sudden change in sunlight—all these things, and so-so-so many more, really do make each photo quite special to me. I continued to post photos in this manner, and after only a year on flickr I had posted more than 15,000 images.

Photography had become my passion, my obsession, my expression of love. Moreover, I became frustrated whenever I missed what I imagined to be the "perfect picture," because exponentially I was beginning to see beauty all around me.

The late great Pop Art artist Andy Warhol perhaps said it first, but the message bears repeating. So, I'm saying it again: if you are an aspiring photographer or artist even—carry your camera everywhere you go, for you're damned if you don't.

I know this to be all too true, because there have been far too many great shots that I've missed simply because I decided to leave my camera behind — usually as an excuse to concentrate on some menial task that I had neglected in the wake of my latest passion.

Alas, I often found myself lamenting the sweet opportunities missed, and each time I concluded that I had been truly amiss with the decision to "just let it rest."

Ah, but there is no rest for the true enthusiast; there is no repose when you are passionate about something and know you have a gift that needs to be nurtured.

When you see, feel, and believe that everything is beautiful, everything is bound to pop out at you and plead for recognition —"Take a picture of me! And me! Me!"—the inanimate will suddenly come alive and provide an endless source from which to appreciate life and create one's art.

And so—you better be ready.

Lesson 3: Use Your Imagination

Man's mind stretched to a new idea
never goes back to its original dimensions.
Oliver Wendell Holmes

Bored and far too exhausted to trek through the city again, one night I decided to use my imagination instead and played with the exposure settings on the camera. As a result, I took several experimental photos that look like skeletons of light.

You see, without the usual comforts of home for three months, I had ample opportunity to employ my imagination to amuse myself. Since I didn't have a TV and was often too tired or restless to read, my greatest source of entertainment ended up being whatever was playing in my head at the time: a trillion synaptic channels rife with blurry memories and murky emotions, fantastic ideas muddled by lurid fantasy, and an incessant profound debate about what I was doing here in this cloister, all alone.

Not to mention, the solitude forced me to use my imagination in the way I approached photography, especially when I went into edit mode.

I soon discovered with great delight that I had a knack for employing what is commonly known as the "cut-out" technique, whereby a photographer focuses on one or a few subjects in a photograph and drains all the surrounding environment of color, so that the focus is clearly on the chosen object(s).

Although this process requires meticulous attention to detail and takes an inordinate amount of time to create, I spent hundreds of hours creating hundreds of cut-out photos over the year that ensued. In a way it became one of my trademark techniques.

Right now, there is a great debate among photographers about maintaining the integrity of photographs, to avoid a certain subjective amount of editing beyond color adjustments.

Yet, how long has black and white been around? After all, we don't see the world around us in black and white. And ostensibly we don't see only one color or only one subject. (Oh, but how we do! It amazes me how much we don't see.)

Granted, most of us with normal vision, regardless of whether we are near or far sighted, pretty much see the same. Or do we? For isn't what makes an extraordinary photograph or work of art special the fact that the photographer or artist has shown us something that they see, but that others had not seen?

Apart from going out almost every night to take photos and then spending countless hours editing them, I made an extra effort to use my imagination when it came to keeping myself entertained, so that I wouldn't take note of the feelings of loneliness that crept up every once in a while.

One night, I bought a big bag of sweet red grapes and spent most of the evening reclining on the air mattress in the middle of the room, tossing up grapes and catching them in my mouth. Another evening I made a necklace out of hanging paper butterflies for my wife, which I cut out of some fancy multicolored gift-wrapping paper.

And yet another, I went into the church after midnight, turned on the lights behind the stained glass windows and sketched them into one of the many empty journals I had either purchased or been gifted over the years.

This exuberant loneliness often carried over into moments when I was alone outside the apartment. For example, whenever I rode an elevator alone, I would enact whatever I was feeling. If I was happy, I would probably dance a little two-floor jig; if I was stressed, my limbs unfolded into fluid Shaolin stances with various insect names—the preying mantis, the flying butterfly, the dung beetle—each a spontaneously generated exorcism of anxiety, the unnecessary pain I was causing myself by taking work or life far too seriously.

It was no coincidence that I made every effort to follow the edict "Use Your Imagination." It was perhaps the greatest lesson my father had ever impressed upon me.

He had those very same words posted in his furniture factory for thirty years, and it was the first thing that his employees saw when they sauntered in each morning.

That is partly why I believe that whether you're making sofas or taking pictures, using your imagination is critical to success, crucial to making the most of what you've already got, and key to making what is good into something great.

For using your imagination allows you to move beyond the singular moment and into the infinite realm of possibility. It prods you into questioning the limits—can this moment merely be a scene or a whole series? Is there a story to tell here? Can this exciting moment be part of a grander adventure?

For the imagination has no limits.

> Some look at things that are, and ask why.
> I dream of things that never were and ask—
> *Why not?*
> **George Bernard Shaw**

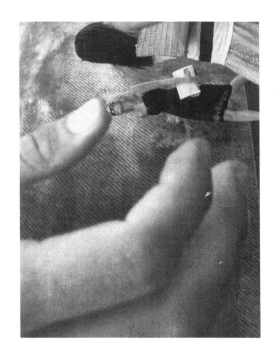

Lesson 4: Take the Long Way Home

When I used to commute into the city each morning from New Jersey, I walked a different path to and from Port Authority, to my office at Park Avenue and 26th Street. My objective was not only to ward off boredom, but also to become intimately familiar with the city.

Sometimes, I'd walk straight across one of fifteen numbered streets between Port Authority and my office, and then head straight down one of the seven avenues: Eighth, Seventh (Fashion Avenue), Sixth (Avenue of the Americas), Broadway, Fifth, Madison or Park. Other times, I'd zig-zag between all the possible combinations of ways to get to and from work. By any and all means, I always seemed to come across something new and exciting.

At the end of my workday, I would wander back to Port Authority to take the bus back to Jersey. Located at 42nd Street and 8th Avenue, Port Authority is right at the edge of Times Square and at the periphery of "Broadway," New York's theater district, so there was always a lot of action going on around that area.

After my separation, I drew on my understanding of the city, of its hidden nooks and treasures, to feed my passion. I also discovered that many of the places I had seen on my way to and from work, were hotbeds for photography. Times Square, especially at night, proved to be a particularly favorite playground for me.

But soon my enthusiasm for taking photos of the city as the sun set right after work and twilight set in before the night— crept up during the day.

When time and work permitted, I would set out to walk in a different direction from my office during lunchtime. One afternoon, during one of my lunchtime photo treks, I came across two sets of splendidly colored windows.

The first included the stained glass marvels inside Calvary St. George's Church at 16th and Park Avenue.

The other set happened to be directly around the corner at 22nd and Lexington at the Collaborative High School, donned

"The School of the Future." Judging by the wonderful tissue paper collages created by the students that I found displayed in the window, I would have to agree.

Despite the sun-worn color of the paper collages at the school and the centennial age of the stained glass at the church, both windows let the sun shine through in all its magnificent glory and I was grateful that I got to take pictures of them.

I was also tickled by the wonderful experience of conjoining serendipity, curiosity, and art. No matter where you live or work or go, there are treasures to be found everywhere. We only have to make an effort to look for them; sometimes it is simply a matter of opening our eyes and senses to see the beauty that envelopes our daily lives.

A good way of achieving this is by trying to see the world through a child's eyes. To do so, you must let go of all the things you must do, and simply explore without an agenda, without the compulsion to keep track of time and place, without a care to divert you away from appreciating all the glorious details of the environment that glimmers around you.

On occasion, we must remind ourselves to think and run and play as freely as we once did, when we were kids, when, as children, we often took the long way home or spun in circles and made odd noises until we got so dizzy that we could no longer stand up straight, so that we spilled ourselves silly onto the grass, and with our arms splayed apart we watched the clouds congeal into giant animal crackers up above, until we caught our breath and our equilibrium again—if only, so that we could do it all over again without a second thought as to how sick we might feel afterward.

I am fortunate to be a father of two wonderful boys who inspire me on a daily basis in this manner. As much as parents serve to guide their little ones via their own errors and experience, children likewise serve to prompt us to let go every once in a while, so that we might truly enjoy and appreciate life. Watching my sons play, I am constantly reminded that kids get in trouble mostly because their organic way of being does not naturally fit into the rigid outline of an adult agenda imposed upon them.

For a number of reasons, I am particularly fond of a photo I once took of my youngest, Dominic, when we were crossing the bridge one late afternoon from Lambertville, NJ to New Hope PA. Not only do the spray of the sunshine, the two levels of depth with the railing to the left and bridge frame to the right and the shadows cast—cumulatively make a richly textured picture, but my son's rattling of fingers against the rail reminds me to "relax."

For the first thing I thought when I saw him doing this was, "You're going to dirty your hands, son!" Immediately realizing how inane my worries were, I let him be and let myself enjoy the moment.

Reviewing photos of my children often reminds me of the adage that, indeed, our little ones become big ones all too soon. It is impossible to over-appreciate every minute of their blossoming, especially when, as adults, we are so eager to regain that blissful state of ignorance and freedom.

Ironically enough, it is the inherent qualities of a child that lead us to the wisdom we often seek as adults. "Wisdom begins with wonder," Confucius once said. Thus, it is through my boys that I am often reminded that it is curiosity that puts us on the path toward such enlightenment.

Far too often, as adults, we forfeit the precious traits that are inherent in us as children—all in the name of fear, conservation, propriety and apathy.

And often for good reason.

But just as often, we do not risk enough, we are not willing to step out of our safety zone, to try something new, to just waste time in the name of frivolity—*to take the long way home*.

As a result of succumbing to the requisite pragmatism of adulthood, we stay stagnant, we diminish our potential, we stop growing, and we proceed down the straight and narrow path until we become bored and unhappy.

This is why we need to nudge ourselves off the road every once in a while, to take a detour without fearing to get lost. If anything, we must welcome the opportunity to see new things, meet new people, have adventures, and most importantly, learn. And by learning, grow wiser via youthful ignorance, precocious restlessness and relentless inquisition about this and that, and this again.

Don't get me wrong. Sometimes we suffer the consequences of our behavior; but other times we find that our circumstances afford us an opportunity to cut a different and unexpected path.

For instance, having the opportunity to live at the Little Church is a good example of how my all-too common circumstances allowed me to draw upon my individual initiative and develop a unique solution.

Like so many others before me, I could either have given in to the notion that divorce was the only real recourse and completely moved out, hired a lawyer, split up the assets, determined custody, and said goodbye. Instead, being that I wasn't yet ready to do this — to simply give in —I made an effort to realize another solution tailored just for me.

In the end, the extra effort paid off because I realized and was reminded of and was turned on to a wealth of awareness about my life, my self, and my passions.

It is true that if it were not for the pioneers who preceded us, we wouldn't have been able to see beyond the thrush. In other words, our predecessors can help us by clearing the way, and thus enabling us to spend more time paving a path toward success.

However, such success also depends upon whether or not we can continue to pioneer on our own, to risk, to innovate and, on occasion—to take the long way home.

Lesson 5: Just Do It

One night I had read for an hour and a half, and I was utterly exhausted. The last thing I wanted to do was to go out and take pictures. It would have been far easier to lie down, shut my eyes and fall fast asleep.

Alas, there was a demon inside of me that prodded me with her pitchfork to pep up, perk up, get out and do something. She whispered, "There's a full moon out there, and you know there's no better opportunity than the present." It was the pull of *la lune* that shook me from my stupor and irked me out of my repose. For I knew that true salvation lies in inspiring oneself and pushing oneself out the door. I reminded myself that I'll sleep plenty in the end, for inevitably we all do.

So, I made myself some strong tea, took a shower and put my camera, metro card and a few dollars in my bag and then took off to Roosevelt Island. Along the way, I stopped by the local market to purchase some water. Then I made a sharp right at the next corner so I could catch the subway at 33rd and Park.

There, as I crossed the intersection, I noticed a giant blinking arrow. Traffic was being redirected for maintenance work. Conveniently, there was a little cove that had been created in the center of the crosswalk by three orange cones. It was there that I crouched and patiently clicked away at what later became the Ghosts of Manhattan, a series of wonderfully enigmatic images that emerged at a slower shutter speed and the dim light of the night.

After taking pictures, I descended into the subway station and boarded the 6 uptown train, but in error, I exited one stop too early. Fortunately, there always seems to be a good reason for making such mistakes; or at least, I usually do my best to create opportunities out of the little crises that occur to me. For, walking around in the wrong station, I happened upon a magnificent colorful wall, where I stood to take more photos of pedestrians passing.

After exiting the subway station at 50th and Lexington Avenue I traversed a few blocks up to the Roosevelt Island tram station at 59th and Second Avenue. On the platform, while waiting for the next tram that would take me over the East River to the Roosevelt Island, I took photos of the buses and cars passing by.

The tram ride was well worth waiting for, because once again I had the chance to take some enchanting photos of what I was experiencing.

When the tram pulled into the Roosevelt Island station, most passengers either went straight to the nearby bus stop or made a beeline past a baseball field and onto where there appeared to be large housing complexes. I decided to go in the opposite direction of where everyone else was going. So instead of turning left, I went right toward the lonelier industrial side of the island, following a road that lie between the river and what appeared to be primarily the back of buildings.

I walked about for about an hour in what was essentially a circle of the back half of the island, taking photos. Despite the fact that the quality of my photos was quite shoddy — dark and muddied — I was nevertheless enamored by the romance of my adventure.

In retrospect, although I genuinely enjoy looking at the pictures, it was the journey, the act of getting up off my lazy ass and getting out to do something creative, new and titillating that moved me most.

I felt that it was only the beginning of many adventures to come, and I immediately began fantasizing about where I might venture to next—all the boroughs with their distinctive neighborhoods, Staten Island, Coney Island, the Brooklyn Bridge, Astoria, Hoboken, as well as any other part of Manhattan where I could walk around and spontaneously take pictures as I pleased.

At 11 pm, when I got back on the tram to Manhattan, I figured I was ready to head home.

However, as I exited the tram and turned around to look at the bridge once more, I noticed the moon hanging there, still taunting me, teasing me, telling me to chase her. Immediately, I knew I would not be heading back all too soon, after all.

And thus, I was off on the second part of my adventure, off to chase the moon.

For a moment I considered getting back on the tram so that I could take photos of the moon while airborne, but decided against it and vied for shots by the water instead.

I started walking toward the East River. Along the way I came across a marvelous red wall and took some long exposure shots with the brick as the side-ground.

I meandered along JFK drive for a while taking photos and eventually turned west until I got to York Avenue. From there I walked south until I came across the United Nations. At 42nd Street I took a few more photos before my batteries ran out and then I knew that, at a few minutes past midnight, it was time to walk back home.

Ultimately, I had had another great adventure. The experience firmly confirmed for me that we must always persevere and *seize the day.*

Seize the day. Do not hesitate, do not procrastinate, the time is now. For it is easiest not to try, to allow all the wonderful moments that distinguish one's own life to go by, if only because—we let them.

It is easy to wander astray and forget the purpose of our aimless wandering. It is easy to dream little dreams that never come true, and to wish to do only half the things others would have us do. And when you want to accomplish something of your own, it is easy to submit to pressure and to act all too indecisively.

It is much easier to follow the mode, the code, to conform, to be the norm and median and the mean, to inconspicuously be all but average and quite unoriginal; to rarely think and simply sit and be amused by others, while unaware of our own apathy.

It is just as easy to lament, to vent, to heave, as you gnaw upon unfortunate circumstance and all that destiny never gave you, instead of grabbing that coveted opportunity, which sheer will and audacious effort procure in us all—the chance to stop the shilly-shally...
... **and positively be.**

Lesson 6: If...

Every night, while I was living at the Little Church, I tried to call home to say goodnight to the boys.

In addition to asking how their day was and inquiring about what each had learned that day, I made an effort to say something meaningful, especially since I was no longer around to read them their bedtime story, as I once regularly did.

Thus, as a substitute for no longer being able to provide the comfort of a nightly, parental routine, I did my best to entertain or teach them something fairly unique over the phone instead.

Sometimes I made up stories about the crazy adventures of my day— "You won't believe this! This morning, I fought off a wild pack of orange monkeys on my way to work!"

Other times, I'd pass on tidbits of wisdom, read interesting passages from science articles, and occasionally, recite a poem or two.

Albeit, I didn't always have their fullest attention because they were rushed as their mother was getting them ready for bed or because they were distracted by something in front of them; nevertheless, I did my best to regularly tell them something of significance, if only from afar, if only "I love you."

One night, I read them excerpts from Rudyard Kipling's incredibly inspirational poem *If.* I used it as a means to teach them, remind them, what I felt Rudyard's words conveyed perfectly—to remain calm at all times.

For no matter what pitch life throws you, you should always be ready to swing. And maintaining one's composure is key to having "the wit about you" to hit the ball.

It was poems like *If* that relayed my values in regards to maturity and manhood while growing up. Unlike some of the traditional values purported in this culture, I felt that composure, compromise, and communication are far more important than any sort of belligerence or ability to fight back.

Moreover, such poetic words helped pull me through my own feelings in the here and now: the painful frustration of not seeing my children and trying to communicate with them as an invisible voice; the venial feeling of rejection I felt each time my words were eschewed by more interesting or present occupations; as well as all the other pangs and pings caused by bouts of regret, guilt, sorrow, and loneliness.

Thus, it was an opening line like "If you can keep your head when all about you, Are losing theirs and blaming it on you" that reassured me that both me and my boys were going to be okay, that we were going to pull through, that one way or another we would take advantage of any and all crises and turn them into unique opportunities to push forward into the unknown, if only because not knowing would be worse than if we had merely wondered "What if?

After moving to the Little Church, over the months that followed while on the streets of New York City, especially at night, I encountered situation after situation where I was to meet danger, daunting risk, and sticky situations and moments that I needed to calmly pull myself out of.

Simply living in New York provided practice for such moments, particularly if you pursued adventures as I had done countless times with various friends over the years. Sneaking on to rooftops, into hidden corridors of public and private buildings, into parties and soirees, as well as persuading doormen to let us in without invitations or being on "the list." There is always something exciting happening in the city, but most of the time you're not invited or you don't have the resources to participate; nonetheless, this has rarely stopped me.

Somehow, in some way, if I wanted to be there, I made it happen, even if I knew it might stir the pot, or that I might have to face questions about the propriety of my presence. Much of the time, me and my partners in crime have gotten away with it and had an extraordinary experience as a result. And almost every time we were able to do so because we remained calm and composed, exuding confidence that enabled us to pass unnoticed.

I have found that time and time again, great photography requires much of the same sort of gall. Not only because it affords you passage into unique situations, but also because it empowers you to take photos that most others would never have the balls to take because they are afraid of what others might say, because they fear the looks they might get, because they shy away from situations where they might appear odd and out of place, where getting in someone's face might lead to tension and an occasional scuffle or two.

Most of the time, although these fears may be very real, if you handle the situation with a smile, with a cocky sort of air that says, "I'm supposed to be here," you can get away with practically anything.

Taking a cue from *If*, even if the sky is falling…hold that lens steady, shoot, and then run like hell and duck for cover.

Point is—remain calm at all times. Learn and practice Zen. Nothing is ever as bad as it seems. Just remain aware, be prepared, and act when your senses tell you to. You can avoid getting run over, incurring upon someone's sensitivities or a trespassing violation as long as you remain calm, cool and composed.

If...
by Rudyard Kipling

If you can keep your head when all about you
Are losing theirs and blaming it on you,
If you can trust yourself when all men doubt you
But make allowances for their doubting too;
If you can wait and not be tired by waiting,
Or being lied about, don't deal in lies;
Or being hated, don't give way to hating,
And yet don't look too good nor talk too wise:

If you can dream - and not make dreams your master,
If you can think - and not make thoughts your aim;
If you can meet with triumph and disaster
And treat those two imposters just the same;
If you can bear to hear the truth you've spoken
Twisted by knaves to make a trap for fools,
Or watch the things you gave your life to, broken,
And stoop and build 'em up with worn-out tools:

If you can make one heap of all your winnings
And risk it in one turn of pitch - and - toss,
And lose and start again at your beginnings
And never breathe a word about your loss;
If you can force your heart, and nerve, and sinew
To serve your turn long after these are gone,
And so hold on when there is nothing in you
Except the will which says to them "Hold on!"

If you can talk with crouds and keep your virtue
Or walk with kings - nor lose your common touch;
If neither foes nor loving friends can hurt you,
If all men count on you, but none too much;
If you can fill an unforgiving minute
With sixty seconds' worth distance run,
Yours is the earth and all that's in it.
And -which is more - you'll be a man, my son.

Lesson 7: Strike a Balance

Prior to the separation, I had long had a regimen where I would wake up at 4 AM to read and write for an hour at each task and then I would work out either in our living room or at the company gym. Now that I was separated and three blocks away from the office, I had a few extra hours that were not taken up by the commute. Ironically, I simply tried to cram in more productivity, rather than attempt to relax a little more.

So to preoccupy my time I began to work out twice a day, once in the morning and once again right after work. In turn, working out regularly allowed me to run away the stress and to keep my mind clear of muddling thoughts.

For many years now, I have focused on trying to strike a balance in life, feeling even-keeled, anchored, despite the tumultuous environment or situation that I might put or find myself in.

Akin to maintaining one's mental composure, striking a balance is the physiological side of being balanced, requiring a constant keen self-awareness of what my body feels.

Apart from striking a balance at any given moment that a situation challenges me physically, it has most often meant finding ways to relax, to get away from the noise of daily life, and to recuperate within the limited time I might have to myself, those spare moments when no one is demanding that I look, react, respond or listen.

The one exercise that I find I have found most effective over the last decade or so is simply a matter of "letting my shoulders down." This literally requires me to relax my shoulders whenever I find that they are hunched up because I am anxious, impatient, or stressed out about something. Other signs that indicate that I may need to check those shoulders include clenched teeth, a furrowed brow, and undulating thighs. Becoming aware of my state of anxiety, however minor as it may seem, and then acting to release the tension, has always proven an effective way to manage stress for me over time.

In addition to managing stress by being aware, as I mentioned before, I practice an irregular form of tai chi, that I like to call "lo-chi," an exercise that I believe plays a vital part in enabling me to strike a balance when I am out taking pictures.

This is especially true when I challenge myself to take difficult pictures where I have to dodge cars, interlock my legs with guard rails in order to lean off ledges a few stories off the ground to take extraordinary pictures of the street, or run away from K-9 units.

Surely, the same applies to anyone taking photos out in the wild, clinging to sharp faced cliffs or climbing steep grades of mountain, just so they can reach the summit and take those breathtaking panoramas of the valley below.

Perhaps, the most important aspect of striking a balance for me however, whether it is while I am exercising, managing my daily stress or out taking pictures, is the realization that one must achieve this alone, that one must strike a balance on your own, from within and that any reliance on someone else to achieve this can only lead to failure in the end.

This morning I was shamelessly seditious. I broke with tradition—and *it felt good*.

At 4 AM as usual, I got up, made myself my four cups of coffee, and began to write and read. But this time, instead of extending my study into the next hour, as I had been doing religiously for the last month, I closed the Dalai Lama's The Art of Happiness and carried my cup over to the living room rug.

I was in desperate need of a rejuvenated exercise routine. And thus, then and there, I refocused all my energies to stretch, meditate and otherwise. But this time, I took a wholly different approach—and *it felt good*.

In the process, I learned a vital lesson about the art of living.

For instead of giving preference to one form of movement or another, as I usually do—I just let go and I moved to the music and my whim as they had me do. Unapologetically, I meshed the disciplined stretching of a veteran runner, faux tai-chi, yoga, meditation, half a year of boxing, and all the energy of the late and great Jack la Laine reincarnated. Essentially, the result was an amazing free-for-all.

But the most liberating point of my work-out was when I integrated dance. I suppose one may misconceive many things about this, in particular, concluding that what I came up with was "aerobics." Au contraire, I truly believe I was a little more fluid than Richard Simmons or Suzanne Somers, as I moved with a kinesthetic intuition honed by years of training that allowed me to unfold into this makeshift routine. Everything from classical ballet to ballet folklórico, from modern, merengue, ballroom, salsa and jazz, and, most importantly of all—all those adolescent years of ecstatic dancing in my room alone—were drawn together for inspiration and a certain emancipation of the soul.

What I gained—beyond a moment of glee, free of the shackles of the stereotypes of gender— was a bit of wisdom that I felt I could immediately apply to everything.

For I learned that one should constantly, consistently break down the limits of all that we learn and allow our intuitions to recombine, so that we end up with a wonderfully intertwined creative force, which gracefully accommodates our natures and takes advantage of the will of the moment.

For over the course of life, we learn to do a lot of things a certain way and quite unconsciously we tend to stick to it, especially if others are involved. So, whether it be how we say things, how we move or how we otherwise express ourselves and engage with others, we often get into a groove of what we are taught and tend to stay there.

And thus, I realized this morning how great it is to just let it all flow organically, so that I might happily recreate for myself *The Way*—with a plié, a sashay and a jiggy—if only because it felt good.

Rejuvenated, I then quickly jumped into the shower, and at six to six I scurried down to the bus stop.

Actually, I ran. And, *it felt good*.

32

Lesson 8: Strike a Chord
(Be Daring)

audentes fortuna juvat:
fortune favors the bold.
Vergil, Aenis

One clear evening I decided to spontaneously take an excursion to a popular spot on the outskirts of Manhattan—Hoboken, NJ, which lies directly across the Hudson.

In one photo in particular, the reflection upon the water was so strong and the image comparable to the light emanating from the buildings, that I whimsically decided to turn it upside down.

Subsequently, I discovered that it struck a chord in me. After posting the photo online, I found that it did much the same for others as well.

The lesson I learned was that it is imperative for one to try to be different, as a person, as an artist, as a photographer.

This is particularly true in the latter case, because otherwise you'll end up taking a lot of staid, boring and bad shots just like every other amateur photographer. And with the dawning of the digital revolution there are a lot of them these days.

One of the more daring methods of taking pictures that I became more adept at and braver at taking was one where I placed the camera on the ground, floor, or street. Perhaps needless to say, I've been kicked, tripped over and snarled at a number of times in the process, but over time I got better at this technique and found ways to be less intrusive and yet still be able to capture the beauty of this unusual angle.

In addition to the mental, emotional and physiological aspects, striking a chord in your life also means striving to be yourself; a self that naturally does not have one side or the other, but rather is balanced by the organic variety of ways that you are compelled to express who you are, who you want to be, who you are becoming as an individual.

This evolution however takes some daring, a bold act of faith in oneself that ultimately will strike a chord in others.

Alas, creativity, success, originality and individuality all require disrupting the status quo, shaking things up a bit, turning up the place, and tuning into one self in order to see things anew.

During our separation, my wife and I began seeing a therapist, Dr. Om Feelgood. We had been to see a social worker before, but that did not work out because, not only did she seem to immediately side with my wife, rather than serve as a neutral guiding force, but she also rarely offered any constructive advice. Her opening question was always "So, what do you want to talk about today," and then we would sit there quietly for a very long minute or two in awkward silence.

Dr. Feelgood, on the other hand, immediately seemed to catalyze each session and offered us exercises that both of us agreed to try and follow. Admittedly, he also employed cognitive behavior therapy, which was much more in line with my own thoughts on how we might resolve our marital disputes and allay the tension.

However, during one session, he actually planted a seed that not only inspired me to pursue photography so passionately, but may have ultimately proved to be one of the reasons I would ask for a second separation a year later.

We were discussing why I spent so much time alone and on the computer. I explained that I had been writing for years and that it was essentially a solitary activity that could not be done alongside someone watching TV or otherwise. I also briefly mentioned that I had taken on many creative projects over the years, and that I had long had aspirations to be an artist or a writer, but had not pursued these goals in earnest because I had taken the more conservative, "do the right thing," straight and narrow road instead.

Just as it happens to millions of others, I began to loop around as I fulfilled the various sacraments of modern life: professional job, marriage, children, better paying corporate job, moving out of the city to suburbia. As a result, I began to take a lot less risks; I began to play it safe, and in turn, my soul began to shrivel—as it yearned to be on the edge, it hungered to be out there venturing into the unknown, it was eager to strike a chord.

In response, Dr. Feelgood pointed out that it is at this age, one's late 30s through early 50s, that many artists actually break out and begin to produce some of their groundbreaking and notable work. Although I had read many books and taken a number of courses about success, genius, creativity and excellence over the years, I hadn't heard of this phenomenon before, and thus I immediately took it to heart.

How could I not be motivated to break out of my shell and finally come into my own, be all that I always had wanted to be?

While I experienced many difficult moments after moving into the Little Church, I have also became more true to my vision of myself. Over those few empowering months I willed and experienced much that is sublime: a transcendence of self, conversations with the divine, ethereal bliss, and the manipulation and making of time; the survival and thriving upon circumstance; realizing a passion and discovering an untapped talent therein; and perhaps, most importantly, realizing that I am in control of my own fate.

When you're willing to be yourself and finally find the courage to be different, your newfound bravery will show up in your artistry as well. I found that since I was taking a bold step in life toward self-fulfillment, that this audacious attitude and determination immediately influenced how I went about and took pictures, what and whom I took photos of, and what I did with them once they were on the editing table.

As a result of my courage, I stuck with things for which I was immediately criticized, including my proclivity toward taking photos of everyday life, my penchant for taking series of photos that "looked the same" to many people, and my "cut-out" technique, which eventually became one of my trademark artistic renderings.

Gustave Flaubert once said that "thinkers should have neither religion nor fatherland nor even any social convictions." One's mind, heart and soul should likewise be inspired by this general principle of evolutionary, pliable and adaptable ambiguity.

Besides being and becoming who we truly are as individuals —being daring, being courageous, not being afraid to strike a chord—also means accepting that our lives are our own, that fate is, in fact, ours to manage and determine. Circumstance, nature, nurture, and all the teachers, authorities, and inspirational figures of our lives merely influence us; they do not hold our destinies in their hands. Only we have that power.

Lesson 9: Don't Take Yourself So Seriously

Learn to laugh at your troubles and
you'll never run out of things to laugh at.
Lyn Karol

My wife and I agreed that I could come home on the weekends to be with the boys, and to give her some much needed relief from the daily care of our children.

And even though I had to sleep in the basement, the inconvenience and discomfort were well worth getting a chance to be with our children, especially when we had a chance to have fun together.

One such weekend, we celebrated my oldest son's sixth birthday. And although having charge of four rambunctious boys in a party mood can drive you nuts, I was duly amused and inspired by their precocious antics.

They showed me how to have real fun: how not be self-conscious, how to be silly, and most importantly, how not to take myself so seriously.

I have long believed that people have problems because they take themselves too seriously. And they take their problems too seriously too. Perhaps it is because some people are simply prone to being melodramatic about their lives, because their lives are not all that exciting to begin with, and so they manufacture excitement by inciting and inviting paranoia, drama, and other emotional hyperbole into their lives.

What most people need more than anything is to unlearn what they've learned, to be less serious about everything and anything that otherwise contributes to their stress, because they futilely attempt to achieve some ridiculously lofty standard.

When you can integrate play into your work somehow, when you can laugh at all your mistakes, when you find yourself smiling for most of the day, then you'll find that you're achieving something worthwhile. If you can't whistle while you work, if you're consistently miserable while you toil, than maybe it is time that you either change careers or change your attitude (at least, until you find a new job).

Many of the most successful people throughout history have actually thoroughly enjoyed their endeavors because quite often they loved what they did. In turn, as they got better at what they did and achieved fame and fortune, as well as received recognition for their talent— the acknowledgement, the accolades and the support often encouraged them to work harder, play harder, and reinforced the belief that they were indeed doing the right thing, and having a good time while doing it.

Over the year that followed my separation, success and recognition of my work began to accrue. Subsequently, demand increased for my photos online, in magazines, at shows, in doctoral dissertations, and even as laptop covers. I began to feel a significant amount of pressure to execute various administrative duties, such as reformatting photos to comply with the various specifications that each magazine, editor or curator required. I had to learn and decide how to print my photos, how to increase the quality of their resolution, how to frame them, so on and so forth.

This not only began to detract from the little time I had to take the photos in the first place, but it also detracted from the pure joy I experienced taking the photos. I quickly concluded that success is not as idyllic as everyone supposes it to be.

I also realized that every once in a while I had to stop taking myself so seriously, that beyond the photo itself not everything had to be as perfect as I would have wanted it to be, or, perhaps more applicably, as good as others were demanding the products created from the photos to be. I had to remind myself that "having fun" was more important than everything else: the accolades, the criticism, the financial gain, the new friends and old ones that began to crawl out of the woodwork.

Many of the most "successful" people in life are also those who enjoy life more than most. Their passion is their play and their play a toast to their passion. There is no such thing as fashion or trends or work for them, unless it is the reason they bend backwards to excuse themselves from the less important demands of others.

Moreover, these exemplars have fun because they ignore, abhor, and abscond socially prescribed ways of expressing their thoughts, proclivities, and personalities. As a result, sometimes they are perceived as strange and unusual, zany and original, individuals who embrace the eccentric.

So let your idiosyncrasies shine through when you take pictures. Don't take yourself so seriously, and certainly don't be afraid to take the opinion of others even less seriously. People like people who like themselves. Your photos will express this if only if they are truly an expression of your self.

Lesson 10: Know Thy Selfe

> Everything that people create is a projection of what's inside them.
> **Stuart Lichtman**

I take a lot of pictures of my kids.

In fact, over the last six years I've literally taken thousands of them. With the advent of digital photography and online photo sites, I can't imagine that I'm alone in this crazy endeavor or that my obsession is unique.

And yet, it has been noticed and commented upon many times over the years how I am conspicuously absent from almost all my photos, children or not.

One weekend while I was home, I went upstairs to the den, which is plastered with photos of the boys, and as I smiled in admiration at all the photos, I could not help but see how wrong these pundits are.

For there, upon these hallow walls, I saw miniature reflections of my self—and there, upon the shelf, the desk, and scattered throughout the house, were indeed cherished images of my little mes. For our children are essentially that, similes of ourselves.

This can be especially true if we love and guide and teach them by our own actions, as to how to be and what not to become.

Of course, they will never be perfect replicas of us, for almost immediately they begin to develop their very own idiosyncrasies, quite often in reaction to what they observe in us.

My boys are by far not the only refractions of myself. For every photograph I have taken has clearly been an expression of me and my outlook and love for life—an endeavor which details the idiosyncrasies of my perspective, of the elected nuances of light and shadow which at a moment's notice pique my senses, of the people and the playful pretenses I delightfully wish to remember, and of all the warm and tender moments in my life, which ultimately have surrendered to a single click of a button.

Be aware that the camera is simply an extension of ourselves, and thus you should take care to have your photos reflect who you are, what you see, and what your life is all about, because ultimately your photos are a visual history of who you are, what you do, and where you've been.

Thus, in addition, to knowing yourself and being aware of how your art is an intimate portrayal of your life, you should know your equipment just as well.

Like the rifle assembly exercise scenes we frequently see in military movies, exact agility and precision are requisites for the adept photographer who must be as agile and intimate with her own equipment as a soldier is with his weapon.

So, know your settings, read your manual (more than once), and practice fitting that hand-held mini tripod over and over again.

When you handle your camera as if it were an appendage of yourself, you will find yourself taking many great photos and far less bad ones.

It took me a while, but after about a year of taking photos of everything and everyone else, I realized that self-portraiture is a good and honest way to get to know oneself. For some it will be easy, but many, if not most, others will shy away.

Regardless, challenge yourself, do not be afraid to see who you really are, and see how others might see you. What's more important than how we look externally is the need to accept that you are this person. And if you don't like what you see, maybe it it's time you make a change.

Another crucial way to get to know oneself is solitude. Everyone should take time to be alone. Time awake by ourselves is as important to rejuvenation as when we close our eyes for the night. In reality, most of the day is a plight of expended energy on others, so it is only during these lonelier times that the truer work can get done, for only then can one think for herself — and not for everyone else who demands her time, energy, and attention.

This is why, when we can close up inside and hide to shut out everyone and everything not essential to our selves, we have the

grand opportunity to focus, to hone in on what is most important
to successful living and ultimately making others happy, because we are equally so.

So to achieve a true self awareness, you must make an extra effort to spend time alone every once in a while. The Dalai Lama does, Ralph Waldo Emerson did; Ansel Adams did; and Edison, Einstein, Feynman, Picasso, Van Gogh, and many of the world's greatest creative spirits and restless minds all knew the power of being alone.

Quite often, after returning from my treks about the city around midnight each evening, I would sit quietly in a church pew, getting to know my long lost self.

Successful artists, scientists, gurus, and photographers all know that solitude is the sine qua non of creation, discovery and epiphany. And for some, the means to personal salvation.

Needless to say, I spent a lot of time alone during my marital separation.

At times I felt a bit lonesome. My isolation was further intensified by the fact that I had decided not to tell anyone— neither family, friends or colleagues knew that I was separated from my wife and that I was living alone in a little church, all but two blocks away from my office.

But as an aspiring writer and photographer, the isolation was quite invigorating and inspiring, for the solitude afforded me much more time and space than ever before. In turn, it became an unprecedented opportunity for me to think, focus and apply my imagination in earnest.

One way or another my strong independent streak demanded that I resolve this situation completely on my own.

Ultimately, I did just that.

Just as the great poet Walt Whitman used to walk alone up and down Manhattan to reflect, photography is also a good way to spend quality time with yourself. I found this out the hard way, in the midst of emotional turmoil, but it nonetheless made me feel quite alive again.

However painful, in the end, my marital separation afforded me a lot of space and photography recharged my life, prodding me to move forward, not backward, in life.

So don't be afraid of solitude—strive for it instead. For less is more. Space, both physical and mental, gives one room to breath, to think, to create, and conceive. For emptiness can lead to clarity, and it is often the optimal conduit for enlightenment and inspiration.

Lesson 11: Go It Alone

"Have you read Don Quixote?"
"I have, and found myself the hero."
"Be so good as to read once more the chapter of the windmills."
"Chapter thirteen."
"Windmills, remember, if you fight with them may swing round their huge arms and cast you down into the mires."
"...Or up among the stars."
Cyrano de Bergerac, **Edmond Rostand**

When I was born in 1967, my parents named me "Lawrence," after T.E. Lawrence, after my father saw Lawrence of Arabia. After decades of playing with my own name, I transformed the namesake into a name that befit who I truly am—Lorenzo, which is not only the Spanish equivalent of Lawrence, but is also the name that many of my older relatives on my father's side of the family have always called me.

So perhaps it is no coincidence that I've long been impartial to loners, those heroic tragic figures who obsessively pursue their passions at all costs, their exuberance enabling them to charm the world about them despite their emotional isolation.

Leaders are often alone in their endeavors. Sometimes they need to recruit, inspire, and persuade others to join them in order to accomplish their aspirations, but from the very start there is this gnawing reality that says no matter how much resistance you meet, no matter how many people say it can't or shouldn't be done as you envision it, no matter what uncooperative circumstances exist—the leader alone must push forward and pull through, until they have accomplished what they have set out to do.

This is one of the most primal and critical motivations for all pioneers, who are often ahead of the pack because, inherently, they have their hearts, minds and souls set on the horizon.

Do not wait for leaders; do it alone....
Mother Theresa

One night, I decided to explore Williamsburg, the new bohemia of Brooklyn. It would be the most perilous of all my adventures —or so I imagined.

At the 14th Street subway station, I was temporarily diverted by one of those performers you so often see underground. He was doing an amusing impersonation of Michael Jackson dancing to *Beat It*.

I noticed a wonderful contrast between the I-want-to-be-like-Mike look-alike and a pretty young lady standing against the rail watching. Immediately, I envisioned that this juxtaposition would make a great cut-out series. And although I also felt it would require hours of editing, I knew that it would be well worth the effort.

After watching the performance I got on the L train and rode until Lorimer Street. Without a map or any sense whatsoever of where I was going, I just started walking and taking photographs.

By the end of the evening, I was literally out in the middle of nowhere, in the middle of the night, all by myself. The flat industrial buildings that surrounded me created an intimidating labyrinth of dark concrete, towering pillars of rusting steel; scattered tumbleweeds of the *Daily News* and the erratic marks of danger were everywhere—cryptic signs of borough toughs with nothing better to do than prey upon innocent photographers.

Each corner seemed like a perilous border of tagging territory, with chain fences ripped apart, exposing gapes big enough for street warriors with big wooden baseball bats to fit through, scrawls of graffiti that warned "Get The Fuck Out, Stupid," and other tidbits of urban hieroglyphics lining every block.

I was wary to say the least.

I nervously crossed a bridge, a small drawbridge over some shallow canal, into no man's land. There were no signs or indications whatsoever as to where I might find one of the bigger bridges that would lead me back into the safer, kinder, better known world of Manhattan.

While walking and looking over my shoulder every few seconds, I realized that New York City is not as small as I imagined. Granted, I knew it was BIG—with five boroughs, 9 million people and hundreds of miles of subway tracks to connect them all—but I had misconceived how well developed the city was—or rather, wasn't; I had imagined that you could walk anywhere and be surrounded by the welcoming warmth of people, of places.

Alas, out here, in the boondocks of industry, there was no such comfort.

Despite my initial misgivings, however, I obstinately kept trekking forward, naively believing that the looping lights of the Manhattan Bridge were bound to come into sight soon.

Yet, after looking at my subway map, which offered merely high-level outlines of the boroughs decorated with a rainbow of track lines criss-crossing sporadically here and there, I inferred that I was really, truly, uncomfortably far off from any such connection to civilization.

Fortunately, as I looked up from my map, a glimmer came into view, and there, seemingly out of the dark blue, a city bus appeared to be coming toward me in the distance, from the other side of the street, apparently, hopefully, heading back to where I had walked from.

Thus, I did the sensible thing and ran across the road to the bus that had serendipitously, suddenly, miraculously arrived from around the corner —Oh, sweet chariot, coming to take me home!

Later on, when I was back safely in my bed at the Little Church, I realized that at a certain point I could have made a wrong turn taking me away from the diagonal direction toward the bridge that would get me back home.

For, as we traversed back over the road I had been taking, it became quite clear how errant I had been, and how lucky I was to be heading back in the right direction. We cruised about a mile before anything residential, anything neighborly, came back into sight, anything that indicated that I might have survived because some compassionate local had come to my rescue, if my worst waking-walking nightmare had manifested itself in the form of a gang of frustrated youth, just as I had imagined for that last two hours.

As we went back over the drawbridge, as vacant lots were replaced by crowded apartment buildings huddled together, as the lights of pizza parlors and bodegas and Laundromats came into view, I knew that I was safe again, and I smiled as I thought to myself, "Next time I'm planning this out with a proper map."

For much of the journey back into Manhattan, it felt like I was alone in the city—all alone in the streets, all alone in the subway station, all alone on the train.

Occasionally, I would see a few transient souls like me, but most of the time it was from a distance. Perhaps than, I wasn't really alone, but merely feeling a bit lonely.

Strangely enough, although I had been admittedly scared during my Williamsburg sojourn, I took comfort in my venturesome solitude and in the inherent danger, because I was doing it regardless of the risks, I was making an effort to do something extra ordinary, seeking out new experiences, rather than simply succumbing to the exhaustion that I tend to feel at the end of each day.

Moreover, while being alone and quite defenseless had its drawbacks, it also had advantages: I didn't have anybody to worry about but myself, I could run a lot faster, trespass a lot easier, and most importantly, take my time. The latter would prove vital to my evolving modus operandi, because I could sit in one spot for as long as I pleased until I felt that I had squeezed all I could out of my photo op. If I had been with someone, I might have felt pressured to leave earlier than I cared to, might have had to bow to resistance to climb fences, sneak through alleys and simply wait as I would otherwise have preferred.

Unless shooting a portrait, I've learned that taking pictures on the street makes for bad company.

For the most part, any earnest artistic endeavor is usually a solitary creative exercise. You must concentrate and focus all your energies on the environment that offers you its aesthetic milk and honey. Otherwise, you're liable to miss something—an angle, a passing fancy, a contrast of subject, hue or form.

Lesson 12: Persevere

One evening, with no particular place to go, I decided to wander around the East Side of New York.

During the first part of the evening, I had a short-lived epiphany, one that lasted all but an hour. For I thought that the hazardous course of my photography jaunts—trespassing, running alongside vehicles, standing in the middle of the streets with my back facing the oncoming traffic—were far less perilous to my person than the liberty I took with my precious camera.

On this particular night, I decided to shoot away amidst a passing rainstorm. Thankfully, the camera survived unscathed.

In the wake of the waning downpour I came upon the entrance to the Queens Midtown Tunnel. I clicked away because I had found a prime position at the sloping entrance and the photos I was taking were exquisite. I was ecstatic and had no time to think about the implications of what I was doing.

Alas, to my utter dismay, others were thinking about the implications of what I was doing.

For out of the corner of my eye, I noticed two patrolmen, slowly, but steadily, approaching me from separate sides of the tunnel entrance. As they got closer, I realized exactly why and what was going to happen. Well, perhaps not exactly, but I had a fairly good idea that I was "in trouble."

They began with routine questions like "What are you doing here?", "Do you have an ID?" "Where are you from?", and "Where do you work?"

Luckily, I was only given a gentle warning and the order to delete the twenty or so beautiful shots I had taken on site at that moment. I cringed as they looked over my shoulder and I went through the stream clicking "erase" on a great set of about two dozen long-exposed photos of bright, perfectly parallel streams of red taillights heading downward into the inferno.

Nonetheless, I was wholly grateful that my camera was not being confiscated or that the memory card was not taken. They read me the patriot act and recited how all photo taking of bridges and tunnels was now verboten in this post-9.11 world.

Moreover and quite amusingly, to the right they showed me a HUGE billboard that read "Photo and Video Taking Not Allowed." I chuckled to myself a little as I relayed to them that I really and truly had not seen that enormous sign (honestly, I hadn't).

As often happens, I got lost in my channeled focus, and tend to block out much of what surrounds me. It is not only a skill you hone when you are set on accomplishing things, but also one that is fairly necessary when living in the big city, especially New York City.

The investigating police officers smiled and let me go after they made sure I understood the gravity of my trespassing by reprimanding and warning me further with, "You know, we could have taken you in for a minimum of 5-10 hours of detention." I raised my eyebrows in response and pursed my lips to show that I was concerned and took their words seriously. Once again I pleaded my utter innocence and ignorance.

Alas, this would be the beginning, for subsequently over the coming months I would be stopped by other police officers for photo taking.

Busted in Bloomfield

The second time I was stopped by a patrol man, it was a little after 1:00 AM, I was literally two blocks away from home, and I had just disembarked from the bus from the city.

A minute after I had gotten off the bus and had decided to take a few long-exposure photos at the corner of the passing vehicles, a policeman pulled up and asked what I was doing.

Hence, as the zeitgeist of our times will dictate, for the second time my name and contact information were written down for "suspicious activity."

Granted, at first, my initial emotional reaction was a bit of frustration, for I immediately began to wonder where this information was going to and what it would lead to—Was I now a suspect on a list of those who take photos of the full moon and street lights? Would I be put on the FBI's black list?

All sarcasm aside, I did realize that this patrolman and the others of the past were only doing their job to serve and protect the people. Alas, that did not help allay my feelings at the moment.

He said, "You can still take pictures, I just have to write all your information down." I sighed to myself in response, and simply said "Thanks," and then put the camera away in my bag to walk up the street to my house. For the joy was gone, as I pondered whether or not I was being placed on some sort of Orwellian watch list.

The "Stupid" Pictures

They say that three times is a charm.

They, whoever they are, are right. For subsequently, I was stopped by a cop for the third time not much time later.

However, this time I received more than merely a reprimand, although luckily less than a citation of some sort.

Apparently, as the stern policeman put it, I had "Crossed the white line for a 'stupid picture.'"

It was a quarter before midnight and I was picking up my mother and my aunt from the airport. Their flight was not scheduled to arrive for another twenty minutes, so I decided to kill some time by pulling off to the side of the road in the back roads service area of Newark International to take some pictures, far away from the terminals and pedestrians and any suggestion that I might be posing a threat to national security. Point being, I thought I would be safe from suspicion or harassment by going away from the real hustle and bustle.

Alas, I was wrong again.

Beyond the boredom, I was also feeling a bit nostalgic. When I was growing up, San Jose, California, was a rinky-dinky town (Silicon Valley was but a twinkle in the eyes of pioneers like Gordon Moore, Steve Jobs, William Hewlett and David Packard) and you could still park directly in front of the end of the single runway that served the airport to watch the planes take off and land, all of them passing closely and loudly directly overhead. It was a cheap form of entertainment, and so my parents would occasionally take me on a Friday night, and we would just sit there for a while watching the planes go by.

I cherish simple moments like that, and so I was hoping to find a little of that again, as well as take a few photos.

So, when I spotted the Budweiser beer factory glowing in the distance, I figured it might prove a nice backdrop against the streaks of light I would get from the cars on the highway that divided the airport from the brewery.

Alas, the world has changed.

A few minutes after pulling my car over, a patrolman pulled up alongside me and asked what I was doing. I responded in the most obsequious and apologetic tone possible and told him that I was taking time-lapsed photos, immediately showing him via the LCD.

He was neither amused nor did he buy my story; rather he asked for the camera, my license, insurance card, and car registration. I complied and added the magical get-out-of-jail free card, the blessed PBA card to the mix.

He sternly replied, "Get in your car while I check things out." I got into my car and placed both hands on the steering wheel and waited.

A few minutes later he stepped up to my window, handed me back everything (almost) and chastised me by saying with a patronizing tone, "Well, it all checks out, but I got you for crossing the white line and riding over the sidewalk. And so I'm keeping the PBA card. You shouldn't have crossed the line for a 'stupid' picture."

I merely nodded tight-lipped and said, "Thank you," in reply.

After he left, I noted "the white line" on the right side of the road, dividing it from the shoulder. I just took his word for it, but until then I was not aware that crossing such a line was illegal. There were no signs to indicate this and usually the un-crossable white line is in the middle of the road parting traffic. Plus his "sidewalk" looked more like an extra-wide curb along side a long strip of dry yellow grass, which so happened to also dip just like a driveway at the point where I entered.

Oh well, either way, I was busted...and all for a "stupid picture." I guess what Forrest Gump said is right, "Stupid is, what stupid does." (Actually, ironically, the truly stupid and irresponsible photos were the few dozen or so snaps I took from

55

the steering wheel while driving 60 miles an hour on the way to the airport.)

Besides, I was secretly proud, that despite the obstacles, the law even, I had persevered.

Perseverance is not only about overcoming the obstacles placed in your way by others, but also about confronting those obstacles that you place in front of yourself. Inherent in persevering is an aspiration to progress, to get somewhere. If you are not moving forward or going somewhere new—you aren't moving at all, and you're in the same place that you've been in for far too long.

> You will either step forward into growth
> or you will step back into safety.
> **Abraham Maslow**

Despite the obstacles, the naysayers, the players that will wile to get their way (and thus stifle yours), one must persevere.

A deluge of dejection due to the flood of rejections, can often overcome anyone attempting to break through and be noticed. It takes a bit of courage to pump up that deflated ego and to keep pressing on, despite the discouragement from the experts and experienced who "know" what will and will not sell.

And selling is paramount these days for publishers, which makes having a "platform" all the more important for anyone who wishes to be chosen as a prospect for consideration.

Without 50,000 e-mail addresses in your contact list, without an established and recognizable name in your profession, without notable accolades for what you are most passionate about—without these qualifications it is likely that your words, photos and work in general will not be deemed "worthy."

It takes a bit of bravery, balls and indifference to rise up from that, to often stand alone, to weather the rejections regardless and to continue creating no matter what.

Ultimately, some of life's greatest rewards come when we accomplish what others say could or should not be done, if only because it has never been done before.

> The art of knowing is knowing what to ignore.
> **Rumi**

Despite the torment though, sticking to your guns, persevering in your own way, usually pays off handsomely. And you feel great about being true to yourself and acting upon what makes you happy. Moreover, people either come to accept your so-called quirks and idiosyncrasies and either end up feeling envy, begin to follow your example or just write you off as an eccentric.

For in 37 years I know one thing is true—perseverance pays off—and it gets you where you want to go, albeit sometimes rather slow-ly, especially when contrasted to all the others who are quickly moving in the opposite direction.

Nevertheless, the will to sacrifice, to stay the course, despite what everyone else might (not) be doing otherwise, has long proven to me to be one of the more meaningful ways of enjoying this short life.

Perseverance is often simply the courage to be different, to do whatever your heart and soul tell you—you should be doing.

Perhaps most importantly, it is vital that you remind yourself as often as possible that you work, you create, and you give your all because you love to; not for any reward, accolades or monetary gain.

It is all too easy to get caught up and lost in these common goals, and subsequently to lose sight of the joy, the nonpareil sense of satisfaction, and the beauty that is your art.

Thus, it is critical that you persevere by reminding yourself on occasion about the original and real reasons that you dedicate yourself to your work.

In sum, one must keep the end-goal in mind, regardless of all that might get in the way and discourage you from becoming a great photographer.

> Doubt is a thief that often makes us fear to tread
> where we might have won.
> **William Shakespeare**

Lesson 13: Be Promiscuous
(Do It Over and Over Again)

Last night I ventured to the Brooklyn Bridge.

I shot 665 photos, and then once I was back in the apartment, I deleted 440 of them, before falling asleep with my camera in hand. I got up four hours later and proceeded to trim that down to 161 photos before going to work. After downloading and editing the photos on my PC, I was left with slightly fewer than a hundred. The remaining set chronicles my adventure to one of the City's greatest landmarks and beyond, into—DUMBO (Down Under the Manhattan Bridge Overpass).

Much as with my other adventures, one of the distinct advantages of using a digital camera is that with a frugal photo size setting (i.e. 1024 x 768) and a larger storage card (e.g. 256 MG, 512 MG, 1 GB) you can take hundreds of photos to document where and when and who and why. In other words, with digital photography it is easy to be easy, to let the moment take advantage of you and to dispense with any prudent inhibitions. This is one case where more is more.

Then again, once you've had your thrill, you have to face the consequences of being a picture whore. More photos can also mean more editing, more storage space, less focus and less time to do other things because you find yourself chimping, chipping away at the photo set like a drunk-monkey, intoxicated by the thrill of capturing so many beautiful moments in time.

Initially, whenever I went on my treks I tried my best to complement my visual documentation of my experience through captions under each photo. Eventually, since I was taking hundreds of photos a night, I decided that one cohesive story would be more prudent and much easier to fashion at the end of the night. Because more is more only for so long, that is as long as you don't feel that *less is more*.

A Bridge Into Brooklyn

I was certain that the evening at the Brooklyn Bridge would be extraordinary because, as I've mentioned before, throughout my life the positive pull of the moon has always shown itself to be a mysteriously magical guiding light for me. Things just happen when there's a full moon out that cannot be explained by science. People get giddy, menstrual flows align, men go crazy with desire.

Thus, with the moon as the evening's guiding light, upon looking up—I saw Her there—and I was bedazzled.

"Oh, glorious moon," I thought, with a tickle of energy swelling up inside of me, a feeling and realization that made me laugh to myself, knowing that this would no longer be an evening cooped up with my books as I had planned. No, now I knew that the moon had thwarted these monastic intentions, because She had greater plans for me.

Prior to jetting off downtown on the green line, I stopped by the office to see if I could catch La Luna against the cityscape from my usual secret cove on the 33rd floor. Alas, she was too aloof.

However, I did catch a glimpse of the blimp that circled my favorite pinnacle, the Empire State Building. It was an amazing sight to see it so up close. I lament (a little) that I am unable to evoke the proximity with the few good shots I got.

After my little detour to the top of my office building, I sped off and down into the depths of Manhattan's metro. To my pleasant surprise I was able to catch the 5 express from the 6 local at 14th street and one stop later I was at the Brooklyn Bridge.

I am particularly fond of the contrast of soft colors in one photo that read "Last Stop," for it has an unexplainable magic ring to it, "Last Stop...Before Brooklyn." And as with all charming moments, people and other phenomena, sometimes it is best not to try and explain, if we want to preserve the thrill that not knowing why or how something evokes.

Sometimes, "it just is," is good enough.

Upon exiting "The Last Stop" I was taken by the first sight I saw as I looked up while ascending the stairs to street level. These vaulted ceilings were bewitching to say the least, and as always, I wanted to take more photos than I forced myself not to take. The glowing green was particularly enchanting, the hue of which I seemed to encounter all the way across the bridge. Not surprisingly, a security guard immediately confronted me and said, "Yo, you can't take pictures here."

Thus, I pushed forward and continued on to the Brooklyn Bridge. This is where the adventure truly began. I had to crouch down once again in the face of incoming traffic, risking having one swerve just six or so inches too far to the right and in turn ending my jaunt as an amateur street photographer.

Although there was much excitement happening ahead and to the side of me, I couldn't help but look back at Manhattan every once in a while in utter awe. For no matter where I went at night in this city, there was always some spectacular display of lights radiating from the skyscrapers that surrounded me.

I imagine that this awesome feeling and appreciation was akin to what people felt a few thousand years ago when they came across the Egyptian Pyramids set upon the horizon of the Sahara. Similarly, I suspect any of the Seven Wonders of the Ancient World garnered likewise respect.

Surely, there has long been something inherently meaningful in the sight of what is monumental. Perhaps, this is the principal impetus underlying the intrigue that pushes tourists through this great city—the natural awe that overcomes one whilst standing before gigantic achievements that are typically not part of the everyday landscape. It is somewhat sad that we are not moved more often to pay homage to the majesty of such things until they have fallen.

Personally, I am liable to gawk at the steel frame of any new metropolitan construction site. The simplicity of a skyscraper's skeleton is as amazing to me as an intricate Escher sketch.

On my way across the bridge into Brooklyn, I took a number of photos of a couple who apparently were coming and going out on the town, taking a wavering promenade across one of the most romantic bridges in the world, back into one of the most lusty and amorous cities in the world.

I was almost accosted by the woman, who leered at me and slurred some irksome slander in a tongue I was not familiar with. It sounded like a sharp Sicilian dialect of some sort.

Her partner wooed her away from attacking me and allayed her enough to shush and press her onward. Apparently they had helped themselves to a bottle of wine at dinner and now she was feeling the emotions that the wine brings out in us all. *In vino veritas.*

Once I reached DUMBO, I walked around for a while, taking photos of the dark alleys, empty streets, vacant buildings and the bridges, which glowed off the water.

I capped my journey with a couple of well-made margaritas at the local landmark dive called Pedro's Bar and Restaurant at the corner of Front and Jay Streets.

I spent a good hour chatting with Coreen, "the bartender." We exchanged life stories, recounting the extraordinary whys and hows and whos that told the tale of why we were both here, at that moment in Pedro's bar.

After I told her about how I was staying at the Little Church, she admitted that she was also staying in an apartment for free out in Queens. She also confessed to being essentially a fake barkeep— she was just helping out the family by serving drinks from behind the bar and had basically learned to mix drinks while on the job. I smiled as I sipped the margarita she had made me, telling her that she feigned bartending quite well.

I lingered a little longer by ordering another round. Although there were other patrons at the other end of the bar, she made me feel like a local by hanging out at my end, casually chatting with me while I nursed the cool green-yellow libation before me.

At half past midnight, I succumbed to my sleepy soul and bid farewell to Coreen and any dreams I had of getting to know her better.

I walked up the block to the High Street station and waited about fifteen minutes before the train came to take me home.

That night I learned that sometimes it pays to be promiscuous, at least with your camera. In other words, there is no harm in trying and trying again, over and over and over— taking lots and lots and lots of pictures, especially if you have a digital camera.

In the year that followed my foray into photography, I ended up posting over 15,000 photos online. I edited every single one of them and estimate that I had taken some 60,000 pictures before editing

Thus, perhaps it is no coincidence that one of the last photos I took was of myself in the window of the Museum of Sex which sits literarily down the block away from my office on 27th Street and two blocks away from the Little Church.

Lesson 14: Take The High Road
(Set Your Own Standards)

During my stay at the Little Church, I also learned the importance of taking the high road and setting high standards for oneself. So that after you've taken 600 photos in a single night, you ultimately end up with a mere handful, a hundred or so that poignantly and truly express what you saw at the moment you took them—and will always make you smile whenever you look back upon them.

I also learned not to let other's accomplishments, rules and motivations dictate your own direction, predilections and limits; because by doing so, you limit yourself from the very start.

Certainly, be inspired by others, learn from others, let others pique, perk and challenge you, but don't let them channel your energy and efforts too narrowly—constantly reach out to new people, be open to new ideas, seek new ways of achieving your own particular vision.

Use your own imagination to determine where you are going, be the arbiter of your own fate, judge yourself. By exploring on your own, you can, and will, determine your very own dreams and aspirations. Rather than relying and borrowing from others, don't be afraid to make your own rules and live by them.

Don't play games. At least don't play them when you could be otherwise producing. I often ask myself, "What am I getting out of the time spent here? What is my return on investment?"

Like television, watching sports, and looking through glossy magazines, playing games, especially virtual ones, is an incredible time-waster. The one exception is when it gives me the opportunity to pass time with someone I love. I notoriously do not like to play board games and it can make me seem quite anti-social, but I often make an exception when it comes to my children, with whom I play chess, Scrabble or poker whenever they ask.

By playing other people's games you're playing by other people's rules. If you have to play a game, play it with yourself—constantly set new goals for yourself and once you achieve the mark, do not hesitate to extend it a little further. And do not be deterred by the detractors who criticize or make fun of you out of envy, do not let them stymie your continual application. Press forward regardless of what others are apt to say.

Besides, if you're going to compete, it is best to always compete against yourself. It allows you to focus and to channel all your energies effectively. By paying too much attention to what or how everyone is doing, you begin to lose sight of your own goals. World-class competitors know that every second, every minim of a moment counts; by being too conscious of the competition you lose sight, you lose focus and you often lose out on the only opportunity to take advantage of every decisive moment.

In other words, don't play by the rules; make your own rules.

William Shakespeare, one of the greatest writers of all time, the granddaddy of English literature, was a notorious rule-bender, rule-breaker, Milo Minderbinder; he paid little heed to the contemporary limits of his language and constantly made up words as he found necessary, and coined innumerous phrases. According to Stanley Malless and Jeffrey McQuain, who wrote *Coined by Shakespeare: Words and Meanings First Penned by the Bard*, Will invented approximately 1500 new words.

Notable literary scholar Harold Bloom goes a step further and points out that Shakespeare not only invented countless new words, but he also essentially invented the human character of the Western canon of literature; and as a result, much of how we learn to be stems from what we read in his magnificent opus of plays and verse, which are rife with human caricature in the extreme.

Essentially, the tome of his plays cumulatively promote the ultimate Freudian joke, a secular self-fulfilling prophesy of sorts with an impact that is proportional to the historical influence of religious texts like the Old and New Testaments and the Koran.

I was reminded of the importance of taking the high road simply by living and helping out at the church, where I was constantly surrounded by symbols, words, and art regaling the importance of high (i.e. moral) standards.

I soon realized that part of those standards included being

wholly honest with oneself, being true to one's purpose, following one's bliss, figuring out how you might best serve your fellow man by acting according to the truth that resounds from within. In other words, to learn the truth, you have to let yourself set your own personal set of standards.

One night when I sat in the middle of the church all alone, with the glowing stained glass windows stationed all around me, I realized how enamored I was by these colorful relics.

The Little Church has what is considered perhaps the oldest stained glass window in the United States; a portrait of St. Faith (Ste Foi) from a Belgian church destroyed in the Napoleonic wars. Taking photos of these windows proved invaluable training by teaching me how critical the subtleties of light are, how important they are to evoking emotion from the viewer, and how they are vital to animating a scene and magically bringing it to life, if only for a moment. I would eventually apply what I learned from these windows to portraiture, which I began in earnest a year after my stay at the Little Church.

The windows I was admiring on this evening were those of the Stations of the Cross, the 14 pictures depicting the Passion of Jesus. As I had done with other windows, I sat there and pondered the meaning of the story illuminated in glass, and in particular what the portrayal of Christ's suffering and crucifixion really meant. For me, at that moment, it became what it meant to pay the price of being honest and being forthright about what one believes in.

Much like Jesus, or Moses, who bore a brutal 40 days and 40 nights alone, without food and water, before God passed on the Ten Commandments, many of those who succeed in pursuing their greatest passions suffer extensively before they achieve or create anything that others might consider worthy of their attention.

> A gem cannot be polished without friction,
> nor man perfected without trials.
> **Chinese Proverb**

This Is My God

One weekend while I was home, I was lying on my back in the kiddy pool in our backyard, admiring the deep blue sky, when I lifted a bright yellow ball with a happy face painted on it, and immediately, I had an epiphany—*This Is My God*—a realization that was perhaps, one of the greatest I have ever had.

An hour later, my oldest son asked me, "Papa, if you could have three super powers, what would they be?"

It took all but a mere moment for me to realize my answer. "Well, first I would want the power to always by happy. Second, I would like the power to make others happy, especially those that are seemingly often angry, sad or otherwise discontent."

Alas, when I got stuck on thinking of a third superpower, Enzo interrupted me and blurted, "No Papa! Those aren't super powers! You have to want powers like 'flying,' 'becoming invisible,' 'shooting fire,' or 'super-human strength'…"

"Oh," I answered, "I guess I don't know than," and lied back again to soak in the sun that was shimmering upon the water, for I had decided that in the pursuit of both sanity and serenity, I was not going to begin a deep philosophical discussion with my six year old—not because he would not fathom its murky depths, but primarily because I knew he would likely take too avid of an interest and interminably ask "Why?" at every turn.

I later realized that the raising of my deity and my response to my son's hypothetical inquiry were indeed, connected.

Because, as I have surmised before, I do believe (indubitably I do) that a strong current of optimism runs through me—one that empowers me to believe in self-actualization, the fearsome force of the individual will, and the belief that there is a little good in almost everyone and everything.

Moreover, if not more importantly, I realized more than ever that perhaps it is part of my purpose in life to share this positive energy with others, if only to alight much the same power in them.

Luckily, I found via this detour of my life that not only did I have a certain purpose and the positive energy in which to fulfill it, but that I also had the tools with which I could express myself and communicate my important message to others. For not only had I honed my ability to write over many years of practice, but now I was adding photography, the power of visual expression to my arsenal.

Moreover, I also had the opportunity to learn how to take pictures wholly on my own. I wasn't going to school, I wasn't depending on erudition or sorting through books on the subject and I had no one to tutor me in the ways of wonderful world of photography. I simply had my will to learn and the yearning to blaze my own path in the process. In addition, I had the streets on which to do so and a lot of extra time in which I could accomplish this new aspiration. There were no tests, no deadlines, and no pressure to achieve any particular milestones. There were no precedents or paragons which I was modeling my work after either. It was merely myself and my senses and whatever piqued my fancy.

As a result, I was creating my own rules and setting my own personal standards as I went along and learned the craft via the school of hard knocks. And I was doing it in the best place in the world to do so—on the streets of fuckin' New York City. School just doesn't get anymore exciting than that.

Fuhgettaboutit!

Lesson 15: Learn to Let Go

Day after day after day, in the midst of my isolation, I began to miss many things—the creature comforts, the conveniences, the large bed to sprawl upon whenever I was exhausted, the immediate accessibility to everything that I had accumulated over the last 15 years of my life—essentially everything that had constituted a home for me, which was practically everything I was forfeiting while separated.

What hurt me most though was not the absence of these material comforts and conveniences, but the loss I felt while being apart from my children.

Even when my wife and I were not separated, I missed them immensely, because the commute to my corporate job in the city from the house out in the suburbs always killed a substantial amount of time that I might have otherwise spent with the kids.

And then, there was the job itself. Although not extremely demanding, most go-getters know that if you are going to vie for any promotion in the corporate world you've got to put your time in, you've got to pay your dues by getting in early and staying late. Otherwise, if you can't demonstrate that you're willing to make sacrifices for the Company, that you're a "Company man," then the Company may not exactly favor you when opportunities arise.

Yet, as your family grows, so do your financial woes and obligations. So, unless you're willing to put the time in, you won't be getting the extra money to pay for them. Being conscious of this certain conundrum, you suck it up and stay late whenever necessary.

Meanwhile, at home, the gradual failing of my marriage was taking its toll. Toward the end, things were often tense and extremely unpleasant. It often felt that every time I came home there was an argument a-brewing, awaiting, a-berating that, ultimately, would make me feel unwelcome. Unfortunately, I began to increasingly feel that it was best to stay away, to find other things to do, such as write (mostly) while staying late at the office, after everyone else had left for the day.

The immense satisfaction I derived from writing, alone, late into the evening, only reinforced my desire to stay away from any situation that would otherwise engender unhappiness.

Ultimately, I do not blame my wife or myself for the disintegration of our relationship, for I found it to be all-too-normal. My parents had divorced when I was 17 and away for my first year in college. When my mother told me what was happening over the phone from 600 miles away, I distinctly remember feeling indifferent; if anything, I felt relieved that now they might stop arguing, that now they might live happier lives apart.

Of course, the transition was all-too-easy for me, being the oldest of three siblings, and being away for four years while my parents transitioned apart from each other. As for my younger brother and sister, I can only imagine how the separation affected them; and in retrospect, I understand how it might have caused some damage. Thus, going forward I had this to consider concerning the fate of my own two children.

Because of the pressure to perform on the job and the looming threat of the end of my marriage—I had to learn to "let go." I had to learn to compartmentalize and to focus on those things that either I knew I had to do or that made me happy. I had to learn to not be emotional about the situation and simply to apply myself resolutely. In many ways, I had to learn to be what our society has traditionally considered to be a "man," one immune to trying situations, one willing to make tough decisions, one who doesn't allow emotions to get the best of him.

So I learned to let go of the idea that my marriage was going to improve; I let go of the fact that I missed the boys woefully; I let go of the anger and the helplessness, and I made up my mind to single-mindedly look forward and never look back.

While at the Little Church, I quickly learned to apply this stoic demeanor toward taking photos. I learned that when taking pictures, you shouldn't be fettered by the lost moment, for regrets may very well cause you to miss the next opportunity.

I learned that letting go also applies to when you're in edit mode. Sometimes you can salvage and recycle and turn trash into a thing of utter beauty, but just as often it is better to just let the shot go and to delete the photo, so you can move on to better things.

One of the fundamental rules of public performance, be it dance, a speech, or a song, is that when you stammer or stumble it is always best to move on. What is wrong can be made right immediately if only we do not pause. For quite often the only person who will actually notice these insignificant flaws is the performer herself.

So, don't let this happen to you. Don't make a mess where there was none—let go and move on.

In other words, forgive yourself. After all, you're only human, prone to err, apt to make the same mistake over and over again.

Forgiveness, allowed me to focus my energies in a positive manner during my separation, so as not to sulk or dwell upon the inconvenience of my situation. By letting go of the past, I was able to focus my energies, my attention and my camera on the making of a better tomorrow.

> Ultimately, to succeed sometimes one must cultivate
> an attitude of gratitude, of giving, and forgiving.
> Nothing can bring you peace but yourself.
> **Ralph Waldo Emerson**

Often for me, looking optimistically toward the future meant looking up toward the sky for positive reinforcement. Whether I was walking the streets of Manhattan, playing with my kids in my backyard in Bloomfield, or on a business trip in Atlanta, simply looking up has always seemed to inspire me.

As a small, yet very important, aside, learning to let go has also meant learning how to let go at the end of the day. Learning to stop working, to stop writing, to stop taking and editing photos, so that I might rest a while. Learning to let go of all that ails me inside: the financial pressures, the loneliness, missing my boys. Learning to let go of my aspirations, to put aside any enthusiasm for a few hours, so that I might shut my eyes and rest my soul, and let my mind repose.

To enable this I try to think of nothing, occasionally chanting to myself "think nothing, be nothing; think nothing, be nothing; think nothing, be nothing."

It is the same principle which underlies most meditative practices, to focus on something rather inconsequential, and subsequently to lose oneself in obscurity, irrelevance, an oblivion that has no time or place—to simply concentrate on the release of tension in your shoulders, the energy buzzing at the very end of your fingertips, the serene emptiness in a sound like *Om*.

> Peace comes not from the absence of conflict in life,
> but from our ability to cope with it.
> **Source Unknown**

To be, or not to be: that is the question:
Whether 'tis nobler in the mind to suffer
The slings and arrows of outrageous fortune,
Or to take arms against a sea of troubles,
And by opposing end them? To die: to sleep;
No more; and by a sleep to say we end
The heart-ache and the thousand natural shocks
That flesh is heir to, 'tis a consummation
Devoutly to be wish'd. To die, to sleep;
To sleep: perchance to dream: ay, there's the rub;
For in that sleep of death what dreams may come
When we have shuffled off this mortal coil,
Must give us pause: there's the respect
That makes calamity of so long life;
For who would bear the whips and scorns of time,
The oppressor's wrong, the proud man's contumely,
The pangs of despised love, the law's delay,
The insolence of office and the spurns
That patient merit of the unworthy takes,
When he himself might his quietus make
With a bare bodkin? who would fardels bear,
To grunt and sweat under a weary life,
But that the dread of something after death,
The undiscover'd country from whose bourn
No traveller returns, puzzles the will
And makes us rather bear those ills we have
Than fly to others that we know not of?
Thus conscience does make cowards of us all;
And thus the native hue of resolution
Is sicklied o'er with the pale cast of thought,
And enterprises of great pith and moment
With this regard their currents turn awry,
And lose the name of action.

Hamlet, **William Shakespeare**

Lesson 16: Make Each Moment Count

> What I do today is important because
> I am exchanging a day of my life for it.
> **Hugh Mulligan**

"There's a truck coming!"

The woman shouted from behind me, as I was taking a photo from the middle of the street.

Although I thought I was fully aware of time and place, her sudden screech threw me off, and drove me to reactively scurry to the other side.

In the process, I bumped into another pedestrian who was crossing from the opposite direction, who likewise seemed to have been jolted into action by the fear intoned in the blurt of this lady's voice. Of course, bumping midway only added to our surprise and fear, so we did a fancy sashay around each other, practically tripping over one another in the process.

Immediately thereafter, I continued walking briskly up Sixth Avenue and didn't bother to look back to see how close we actually had been to being hit, struck down, or crushed by the speeding vehicle that had prompted the concerned stranger to yell out.

When taking photos I often sought perilous adventure—standing in the middle of the street with my back to the oncoming traffic; literally running through the streets to take photos of taxis, buses, bicyclists, and even skateboarders, in action; and going to a lot of places that I shouldn't have, especially alone, especially at night.

Sometimes I felt as if I were playing out my midlife crisis. For immediately after my separation—I took up photography and became much less averse to risk than ever before.

I think ultimately a lot of men like myself place themselves in such danger because they are trying desperately to make life count, drumming up meaning via adrenalin and testosterone-abetted actions that court peril, and thus make us feel *Alive Again!*

> Life is not measured by the number of breaths we take
> but by the moments that take our breath away.
> **Unknown**

After the truck incident, I did once again have to wonder why I put myself in danger so often these days. I have foolishly convinced myself that I am agile enough to avoid an accident. Yet, at the same time, I always end up questioning the sagacity of this reasoning—close calls almost always thrust me into an inner debate, so that on the one hand, I'm grinning with glee as I congratulate myself on being so brave. But on the other hand, I am also thinking, "Boy, you're really stupid..."

And almost every time, I try to convince myself that I have to quit this game I am playing with my life, berating both my id and ego with "Now, this is the last time you two! No more monkey business."

Only problem is that I'm all too human, and boredom follows me everywhere—so that everywhere I go, ennui seems to go there with me.

Hence, my futile attempts to shake her by jumping into the middle of traffic, dodging busses and running along skateboards to get some stupid picture.

They say luck is a lady. If that's true than I love her, and I feel that she loves me, but that doesn't mean that she ain't going to leave me someday.

On the other hand, I never knew photography could be so much fun, so utterly fulfilling, invigorating and absolutely—life affirming.

At the beginning of Niezstche's *Thus Spoke Zarathustra* a tightrope walker plunges to his death. The following conversation ensues between Zarathustra and the fallen, prior to the latter's last breath:

> "By my honor, friend," answered Zarathustra, "all that of which you speak does not exist: there is no devil and no hell. Your soul will be dead even before your body: fear nothing further."

78

The man looked up suspiciously. "If you speak the truth," he said, "I lose nothing when I lose my life. I am not much more than a beast that has been taught to dance by blows and a few meager morsels."

"By no means," said Zarathustra. "You have made danger your vocation; there is nothing contemptible in that. Now you perish of your vocation: for that I will bury you with my own hands."

To die by one's vocation—that to me is perhaps the highest form of passion. To live and perish in the thrill of one's purpose and the moments that made life meaningful for you as an individual. That is the ultimate form of living. And perhaps, it is living dangerously, but it is also living.

How many heroes have done much the same? Those we hold in the highest esteem live and die by that which they know to be their calling.

9.11 and the bold acts of all the servicemen that perished is a poignant example.

Just the same, the artists, writers, scientists, entrepreneurs and other elite minds and imaginations who died of old age are equally laudable, because they held their course in life, and quite likely had to overcome countless obstacles, defeat numerous monsters, and outwit conformity, complacency and their seven ugly sisters: jealousy, envy, "virtue," materialism, righteousness, apathy, and the unknown—often, alone.

The greatest journeys are always alone and end with death, which is why the journey itself should be the ultimate goal. Fulfillment comes with the fulfilling. If you are constantly looking to go somewhere in order to achieve happiness, you'll really never get there.

To my fellow adventurers, my fellow photographers, I say Make Every Moment Count!, as well as its corollary—Make Every Shot Count. Position yourself well, and then click before you've lost the nerve.

Life is fleeting, as are all the fine moments that cumulatively constitute our existence.

Lesson 17: Weather the Elements

One rainy evening, after wandering around Greenwich Village taking pictures, I took the M60 bus uptown. I ended up on the bus alone, all the way up Sixth Avenue. I couldn't help but question what I was doing here in this desolate place and time of my life.

At one point I swiped my hand across the foggy glass to take a peek outside, and instead I saw my reflection in the water-streaked window. I smiled and chuckled to myself, for I realized that although I might have felt a little lonely, I was making the most of my situation. And, actually, having a rather spirited time of making the most out of it.

"Neither Rain Nor Sleet Nor Snow Nor Dark of Night" is etched in stone at the top of the main post office in New York City.

Good photographers likewise should not fear the elements. Whether it be nature when she is being naughty or police officers merely doing their job by enforcing the law, a strong photographer will roll with the punches no matter what storm circumstance suddenly throws at you.

And for that reason, when everyone else is cowering inside, or huddled under an umbrella—you, my astute and brave photographer, are positioned and ready to take great photos.

One evening, I realized how wonderfully conducive the rain actually is to taking photos. I was sitting under a wee bit of awning on Canal Street, on the border between Chinatown and Little Italy, with my hooded poncho and baseball cap, patiently waiting, while people scurried like ants being taunted by a precocious six-year old boy. The result was a slew of great photos that showcase the beauty of the rain swept streets in New York City.

> For after all, the best thing one can do
> when it's raining is to *let it rain*.
> **Henry Wadsworth Longfellow**

For the first month while living at the Little Church, I ventured out into the warm rain almost every evening regardless of the spring showers. The experience was incredibly fulfilling. For sometimes, as the hoi-polloi huddled indoors, it felt as if I had the great metropolis all to myself.

And sometimes, through photography, I felt (and often still feel) that I have the whole world and this wonderful life all to myself as well; seeing what others so easily overlook, often because they are too busy or too tired or scared to pause and take notice.

One of the best-known scenes from the wonderful movie musicals of the 1950s is when Gene Kelley dances and sings his heart out in *Singing in the Rain*. I've watched that scene repeatedly over the years, and it inspires and moves and motivates me—each and every time. The man is in love and he is happy and he has the sudden impulse to dance and sing; and despite convention, and what others might think of him, and the fact that he is getting soaked, he does exactly as he feels he should be doing.

It was this kind of feeling that pushed me out every night; it was a feeling that I have carried through most of my life, and one that I was feeling free to express once again—and oh, what a feeling it was.

83

Lesson 18: To Tell The Truth

For many New Yorkers, the death and tragedy of 9.11 opened up our eyes and hearts to the truth and beauty of our lives.

On September 11, 2001 I was in my office on Park Avenue when all work stopped. Suddenly all eyes were glued to the television, as planes crashed around the country. Every moment was incredibly tense. You couldn't help but ask yourself, "What the hell is happening?", "Are we next?", "Is this Armageddon?"

Across the street from my office, on the outside wall of the local 69th Regiment Armory that was initially set up as a missing persons registry, friends and families of those who lost their lives in the Twin Towers began putting up hundreds of missing person fliers with the last photo they had of their beloved lost, many with tear-jerking and heart-wrenching questions like, "Do you know where my Daddy is?"

Although the concentration of these notices were at the armory, they were also posted everywhere on the streets, on lampposts, bus stop kiosks, mailboxes, and public telephone booths. And so we saw these reminders of that tragic day everywhere, everyday for months afterward. Needless to say, the massive demonstration of loss and lament, of mourning and the vestiges of hope, had an indelible impact on the psyche.

Almost immediately, people became quite cordial with one another again. Many of us now felt, as we accidentally looked into strangers' eyes, a certain connection, a definite realization that made us all human again, and not simply some hurdle preventing us from getting to where we were going.

For those first few weeks, whenever you inadvertently made eye contact with people you passed on the street or in the subway or on the bus, you were in a sense saying "We survived, we are alive," and somehow, in some strange morbid way, this connected us. It is a truth that most of us overlook almost everyday, and unfortunately it took the events of 9.11 to break open the hard shell that we wear when we trample indifferently through the metropolis, each step cold and calculated, because otherwise every bink and bonk, clink and clonk of weathering caused by modern life would wear us down.

Yes, tragically it was the sudden loss of thousands of lives that reminded us that despite our inclinations to ignore and suspect and retreat from every stranger we see, ultimately both dead and alive—*we are one.*

My separation also made me feel that the shell of our marriage of make-believe had been cracked, and that the truth underlying our relationship was being exposed and seeping out.

Part of that truth included the fact that I missed my children immensely as a consequence of my ousting. I was compelled to call them every morning and every night to convey this heart-felt truth to them, a truth that was most often best conveyed by simply telling each of them—"I love you."

> Kind words can be short and easy to speak,
> but their echoes are truly endless.
> **Mother Teresa**

The truth that I realized over the following year was that in order for me to be happy, in order for me to provide my children with the best love possible, I needed to follow my bliss, I needed to not only tell my children that I loved them, but I also needed to show them how much I loved them by demonstrating that I love life and people and adventure and being creative. Because I came to realize that to love your children is to show them how to live in the best way that you as an individual know and yearn to live.

Thus, with this ideal in mind, I was quite restless the entire time I was living in the Little Church. Hence, the thousands of pictures, the countless words to describe my experiences, and passionate effort I made to learn this new art. Every time I felt either the pangs of their absence or the pain of guilt for not being there with them, I consoled myself by remembering that if I can show them how to extract the most from life, how to live and be extraordinary, then, hopefully, I will have gone beyond the normal, common call of parental duty.

Regardless of the truths I have realized through loss, I have also long known, and adamantly believed, that truth is relative.

We fashion reality, for ourselves and for others, everyday, with each new perspective that we offer through our words, through our opinions and recollections, and even through our photos. For what we choose to photograph is merely a manifestation of what we value, what we deem special enough to us, if only at that moment, to remember via a picture, and perhaps to eventually share with others.

Being conscious of this, I have made an extraordinary effort to see things and situations and environments in more ways than one, especially when I take pictures, especially when I venture out into New York City, which, with more ethnic populations than any other city in the world, is in and of itself an exemplar of how diverse truth can be.

It is mind-boggling to me to hear people say that there is only one truth, one right way. Throughout my life I have met and known a lot of people who see the world and life as divided between black and white, good and bad, right and wrong. On the contrary, I see truth as something, somewhere, in between.

Life is rarely, if ever certain, for everyday we are blessed simply to be alive. And by keeping this thought in mind I am motivated to make the most of every opportunity, to seize the day and live life my way, by always seeking the truth and being true to how I feel as an individual.

Understanding, and most importantly, accepting, the relativity of our existence has long been a means of maintaining my sanity, my optimism, my composure, and most of all, my happiness. This mindset allows one to be flexible; allows one to seek a better, fuller, understanding of why people behave as they do; allows one to remain calm at all times; and it also allows one to change and adapt with each turn of events, with each surprise, with each change of plans, and with each relatively minor disappointment.

For disappointment is generated because of our mindset, that is—how we see and perceive and feel about things and situations and people (and their actions, or inaction); it is in other words, *a relative truth*.

Thus, whenever we feel any negative emotion because of others or because of our differences with them, because of the clash of truths that arise from the congress of realties, it is incumbent upon us to see the situation differently, so that we do not let the situation impede, impose upon and hinder our lives somehow. Either we must learn to compromise (often), accept the situation and be happy with it, accept the situation and move on, or make an effort to see it differently, in a positive light.

Perhaps more vital to living a happy and healthy life though, is our ability and willingness to act once we've realized a more positive truth. This is the hard part. Seeing things differently is one thing, doing something about it is another.

> Vision without action is a daydream.
> Action without vision is a nightmare.
> **Japanese Proverb**

Sometimes (sometimes) telling the truth is the best way to set up wonderfully candid and honest shots of others.

To my surprise, I've found that strangers usually concede when you plead and woo them with a little flattery and a wink to soften them up—"Oh, I just have to take your picture! Your eyes are absolutely gorgeous!"

But the real secret to their concession is that you actually mean it when you say it. Although using faux praise is a definite faux pas, don't ever hesitate to express yourself whenever you suddenly feel something positive, whenever you notice something about someone that (aesthetically) tickles you somehow. And don't forget to ask to take a picture in the process.

This tenet sounds so simple, yet it actually is one of the most difficult things to overcome when taking pictures of people. For most of us are naturally prone to be wary of strangers. We have been taught to either not let people take photos of us or not take photos of others because, somehow, it is invasive.

But if your enchantment with a potential subject is genuine, your sincerity will shine through and you will likely be granted a pass to take that special photo.

Moreover, it is important to keep in mind that beauty is in the eye of the beholder. "Beautiful" need not comply with its conventional meaning. If something about a person caught your eye, something out of the ordinary, something shiny and new, something warm and blue, then it will likely not be difficult to convince this person to submit to your camera, as long as you convey your appreciation with utter and immediate sincerity.

Speak literally.

Say what you mean without justification, without any desire to manipulate, and without concern about how another may interpret your words.

Practice not being careful.
Experience the freedom this brings.
Byron Katie

Lesson 19: Believe in Yourself

Are You a Photographer?

It is very important that you strongly believe and enthusiastically answer "Yes!" to this frequently asked question.

From the onset of any adventure, any individual initiative, any effort where your ego is at peril, you must strongly believe in yourself and what you've decided to do, regardless of the risks, regardless of the ridicule.

Most of all, it is vital that you are ready to exuberantly take on whatever comes your way with unfaltering optimism. You must think, "Anything is possible!" Champions do, winners do, Olympians do, pioneers do, many, if not most, of the successful people in the world do—so why can't you?

And regardless of your status or lack of compensation for your photography work—or any other passion—your heart should not skip a beat when you reply affirmatively to the question.

A sincere smile, one that folds inward to warm you, is also a great way to punctuate your answer. Smiles are one of life's greatest weapons, for they can make practically anyone feel welcome and immediately disarm anyone of their fears, paranoia and reticence.

Even if no one is paying you to take pictures, you need to take them in earnest nonetheless. For a genuine effort is what helps raise what you do to the level worthy of your time and effort. Otherwise, you might as well put down your fancy equipment and be satisfied with using a Polaroid or the ubiquitous camera phone.

And so, when the curious begin to prod and ask: Where? When? For whom? Don't be ashamed to explain that you are an avid amateur photographer.

Equally important to having the confidence to call yourself a photographer is the feeling that you are a photographer, if only because you love the craft.

> You are never given a desire without also being given
> the power to make it come true.
> You may have to work for it, however.
> **Richard Bach**

I have always been blessed (or cursed) with an overabundance of confidence, a stalwart constitution, and an overly optimistic demeanor, so that "reality" has rarely been a deterrent for me.

As I grew older and more experienced, I realized more and more that reality was in my realm of influence, reality was wholly relative and could be fashioned to my liking—reality was whatever I wanted it to be.

Thus, dreams could come true, if only I was willing to make the sacrifices necessary to enable them; if only I was willing to give up many of the things that others take for granted like sleep, rest and time for leisure and languid hours spent doing absolutely nothing; if only I was willing to focus and put all my energy, enthusiasm and attention toward the task of designing and executing my own fate.

Moreover, it is vital to understand that this vigorous mindset always applies to both the big picture, as well as the smallest situations. If you are a participant, nothing is ever out of the reach of your influence. You are never a victim, if you can be blamed for not making an effort.

Directly across the street from where I had been stopped and questioned by police in front of the Queens-Midtown Tunnel was a local dive serving up extended happy-hour $5 margaritas. Feeling a bit frazzled, I felt that my photo taking was essentially over for the evening, and thus, I thought a little lime, salt and tequila would serve me well and put me at ease.

I was served by a pretty bartender, whom I decided to photograph. As I began taking shots, she initially reprimanded me, asking with a taunting tone, a furrowed brow and a squint in her eyes, "Are you taking pictures of me?" I thought for a split-second that I should lie, but decided it would be best to reply otherwise, and thus answered honestly, "Why, yes, Ma'am. I most certainly am taking your picture."

Her tone suddenly softened and she further inquired, "Oh, are you a photographer?" And once again, for a split second I had to consider my answer. "Am I a photographer?" Having just been harassed for not playing by the rules, for attempting to once again capture the beauty of movement that pulsed through the metropolis regardless of the daunting circumstances, I realized that "Yes, I am a photographer," and thus answered affirmatively.

To my utter surprise she then smiled and said, "Well then, click away."

I intuited that much like so many others working the night-shifts in this town she was an aspiring actress or artist of some kind. She confirmed that she was indeed the former and proceeded to demonstrate her acting agility by not-so-subtlety posing for me, quickly changing from being a demure or paranoid stranger one moment to a garrulous photo-whore the next.

In the end, once again, I was elated that I had decided to speak the truth, even if it was only my relative truth of the moment. I had the balls to believe in myself, despite having just had my ego deflated moments earlier across the street.

Moreover, I knew only failures gave in after falling the first time. Too many people just quit after failing after the first try because they immediately lose their self-confidence. Winners never concede to circumstance, they just keep on trying and continue to believe in themselves and in their aspirations. And ultimately, they become whatever it is they believe to be true. For faith in oneself is the first step toward truth.

Whether you think you can or think you can't, *you're right*.
Henry Ford

Lesson 20: Steady as She Goes

As photography immediately became part of my daily routine, it also soon served as my emotional and psychological anchor. Taking photos was a wonderful catharsis; it became my shrink, my religion, my crack and my shot of insulin. It provided me with something I could hold onto while I was sailing across the tumultuous sea of my separation.

And I don't think it was a coincidence that I was taking refuge in a religious sanctuary either, a House of God, where millions of troubled souls before me had sought solace, meaning, and often, simply something to hold on to for a rejuvenating moment of repose.

As I'd mentioned before, photography initially served as an apt substitute in the beginning to something else that had served as my compass, my balance beam, my middle ear and my leveler—writing.

Almost immediately I found that both arts complemented each other perfectly; and as a result I feel that I came back to life twice as strong, twice as aware, twice as caring and daring and willing to pursue my dreams and all that seemed right to me, regardless of how wrong it was to others.

The Sun itself also proved an indefatigable mental anchor for me as well. Because, inevitably, if I was ever feeling a bit down, all I really needed was some sunshine to turn my frown into a smile.

More so, this occurred whenever I had an opportunity to take pictures of the glory of the sun shining upon New York City. It was a particular thrill for me to stumble across an alley, a street, or some crevice in the concrete canyons that let the sun shine in just right. Oh, what a delight it was to be there, to take photos, and then to show and share them with others.

There are so many things in life that can and do serve as anchors to us: our heritage, our family, our friends.

But apart from the more tangible elements that help stabilize and center our lives on the outside—ideals, values, and passions provide much the same for many of us internally.

Then there are such things as nationalism, patriotism, religion, sports team fanaticism, and so many other "isms" give meaning to our lives, yet do so for artificial reasons. For the traditions, rituals, ordinances and beliefs of all these often require that the individual rely on what others have already determined to be the prescription for behavior and thought, rather than trying to figure it out for themselves.

Granted, it just makes life easier to simply accept what we are taught, but ultimately it does not make it more fulfilling.

Ultimately, it is most important to rely on your gut feeling — that anchor within — when it comes to deciding what is right and wrong, left and right, upside down or inside out for whatever situation you are in, at any given moment. There is much more stability in mental flexibility and moral ambiguity than when one has "it all figured out."

And it was the anchor within that had placed me where I was now. After many years of neglecting that gut feeling, I had finally listened and knew that somehow I had to move on.

Unfortunately, there is a misperception, a misunderstanding, an utter ignorance of the fact that people still grow as individuals throughout our lives, even, if not especially after, we decide to try and share our lives with another wholly different individual.

Alas, there are too many pressures for us to remain the same, the conformity of which only makes us feel ashamed and ultimately unhappy, and leads to the seemingly endless rally of arguments and petty misunderstandings.

If only people understood from the beginning of their lives together that each person still needs to grow and pursue avenues alone sometimes, than maybe this marriage thing might work for more people than there are actually vying to stick it out these days.

For the truth is, times are changing and we are seeing a much greater diversity of what it means to be a "family" today than ever before. We are also seeing more people wait to get married, more young people willing to explore what maintaining a relationship means or who they should have relationships with, and more people ultimately deciding to stay single for their entire lifetime.

Also, although the advent of the Internet has made matchmaking more efficient, it has also become the bane of dating, because it raises the bar and increases our expectations unrealistically. For people are less willing than ever to compromise, to wait a little longer and to tolerate the idiosyncrasies of others, because they can always "find someone else." Ultimately, it merely feeds the fallacy that there is a "soul mate" out there waiting for you.

So, yes, there may be others out there who are much more akin to who you are. And, yes, the Internet combined with algorithms may afford you the opportunity to find them.

But in the end, there are always differences, some twenty to thirty years of whole childhoods, periods of tumultuous adolescence, and increasingly reclusive adulthoods that have influenced and formed who we are and who we continue becoming.

If we are marriage-minded, we must accept and expect that it should take just as long, twenty to thirty years as long, before two individuals can come to terms with one another in marital harmony. And it is then, and only then, that you can really, truly, begin to grow together as one.

Thus, it was during my separation that I realized that my wife and I had roots that were anchored in totally different terrains. Eventually, I accepted that our different sets of values and ways with which we went about dealing with life fated us to grow apart.

Ultimately, I realized that I had to depend on the anchor within once again, I had to deal with the circumstances that were taking away many of the creature comforts of life and I had to focus on the pursuit of happiness via my passions for writing and photography.

If you always rely on yourself to maintain your emotional and cognitive equilibrium you'll always be equipped to pick up your internal anchor and move on to wherever the winds of life take you.

Otherwise, by depending on others, you're liable to get stuck in the mud.

Lesson 21: Eyes Wide Open

While living alone, waking up alone, going out to take pictures alone, eating alone, being alone I became much more aware that I was not alone, that apart from other people, the world was full and overflowing with life, with beauty in motion.

There is a set of photos I took one morning, where I ended up capturing pedestrians passing by a bright blue wall and some red garbage dumpsters.

After a second look at this set I noticed a distinct pattern amongst the pedestrians—almost all of them were "tuned out." Either they were on the cell phone chatting away or shut out from the cacophony about them with their headphones on and iPod plugged in.

Through photography, I not only learned that you should go about your business always in tune with your environment, opening your eyes to its beauty, but you should actually, literally, practice taking photos with both eyes open.

Seemingly, it is "natural" to shut one eye so that the other might focus via the viewfinder.

However, although visually this is true, our brain has the capacity to see more. By keeping the other eye open, you gain critical peripheral vision, so that you capture that passing fancy just right, at the right moment.

I also learned that it was a good practice to take a few dispensable practice shots first, so that I could get my timing, angle and leveling down just right.

Alas, LCD displays might make this little tip all but obsolete, just as the digital camera itself is shoving film cameras aside.

Nonetheless and allthemore, keeping your *eyes wide open* is a great mantra for a full and meaningful life—for most people go about life with their eyes half closed.

Lesson 22: Everyday is Extraordinary

One morning, I woke up and decided that from that point forward I had to do something apart from my daily routine, something extra ordinary each day that would improve my life, if only in some small way.

It did not matter how minor the task might be, for ultimately, if it made a fraction of a difference, it was good enough for me.

One evening, I organized my closet—sorting suits, arranging shirts by color, lining ties up, so that they lapped neatly one over the other. An orderly wardrobe had long been a priority for me because I didn't like to waste time deciding what I wanted to wear for the day. In fact, I often chose my outfit the evening before and assembled it together on the rack (I've long wanted to take this a step further by buying a dozen of the same shirts, suits, trousers, socks, and shoes, as well as making them all black—or white, so that I would never have to think about matching again.)

On other nights, in the expedition to find all the little things that count, my efforts sometimes flew off on delightful, albeit brief, flights of fancy.

I might satisfy an urge to go to the deli around the corner and try something new; thereby consciously expanding my horizons, and contributing to exposure and experience of the multivariate magnificence that is life.

Sometimes this effort meant taking up something slightly more serious. For example, instead of venturing out to take photos in a neighborhood where I had never been, I would stay late at the office searching for sites where I could submit my work.

After all, if everyday is extraordinary, then you have a chance to be and do something extraordinary, every day.

Although, it is natural for us to lament the doldrums, the banality, and the ennui of our existence and seemingly the grass is always greener on the other side, in reality, it is often just as green, if not greener on our side. Just take a look around you; whether you live in a small town in Ohio right off of Main Street or in the projects of Morningside Heights Manhattan, our surroundings are rich with photogenic opportunity.

Often, it is simply a matter of widening our perspectives and making an effort to make something out of nothing. For everyday is truly extraordinary, if only because we are healthy and alive and astute enough to see the glory of the sunrise and the stark beauty of all those things we take for granted.

> There are two ways to live your life.
> One is as though nothing is a miracle.
> The other is as though everything is a miracle.
> **Albert Einstein**

I often get this feeling whenever I walk through the streets of Manhattan, for it is so easy to overlook all the amazing architecture that the city has to offer. Day in and day out, it may all seem the same, but that is only because we rarely take the time to see how special each building, each gargoyle, each marvel of modern architecture truly is.

The truest and most worthy form of appreciation of any creative work that merits aesthetic recognition, would be to appreciate it for at least as long as it took to create it, if not longer.

Perhaps we come closest to paying such things the respect they deserve when we play a song over and over again, at least until something, or someone, new catches our attention; or when we give it personal meaning by attaching it to a ritual or fond memory in our life.

There will always be an inherent, and quite normal, imbalance between the effort that was needed to render a moment of inspiration into a relatively permanent manifestation of glory—some call this art—and the energy with which we enjoy the results of the artesian, artist or architect—via rather hurried museum glances; the slow dances to the music that is merely the conduit to the more dynamic art of romance (i.e. love in the making); or the rereading of a few passages from an inspirational book.

This skewed relationship between the energy endowed and the cursory effort made to extract its meaning is like gleaning merely the glimmer of that light which glosses over an epiphany. It is this disequilibrium that leads us to awe.

This is why the Sistine Chapel, the cathedrals of Notre Dame, the Taj Mahal, Mecca, the pyramids or any skyscraper that scrapes the sky—all implore us to sigh and bow before them. Everything from these architectural wonders to simple love songs, insightful verse and our greatest epics—are all works that we take for granted all too readily.

We may not need to spend time paying homage or genuflecting or praying in their general direction to duly appreciate these magnificent works—these marvels of architecture, the buildings that make the metropolis of New York one of the greatest cities in the world— but we should occasionally, if not often, acknowledge how incredibly fortunate we are to know them, to pass by them each day, to walk in the shadows of such giants; and moreover, to be moved both by the small and gargantuan efforts of the men and women who created them.

For life becomes quite amazing—when you realize how truly amazing it really is.

Lesson 23: Envision

>"Much of life becomes background, but it is the province of art
>to throw buckets of light into the shadows and make life new again."
>>*A Natural History of the Senses,* **Diane Ackerman**

Photography became such a satisfying pastime for me during the separation that I began to envision, more than ever, how I might have a fighting chance of succeeding at being and becoming an artist.

However, first, I had to overcome my own prejudices; I had to accept that I could actually become an artist before I could actually make an effort to do so.

Ironically, although my father may have been a major proponent in this regard (i.e. "Use Your Imagination, Son") he was also definitely one of its greatest deterrents.

But I don't blame him. Far from it.

For although he discouraged me from pursuing a career in the arts, he and my mother also provided me with all the financial and moral support I needed to attend a prestigious college prep and to go on to college, even as they were divorcing during my freshman year.

And if it hadn't been for my high school years and my sophomore literature class in particular, I wouldn't have read James Joyce's *Ulysses,* and I may not have been inspired to be a writer. Because even though I did not understand a lot of the arcane references at first, the intricacy of his words set me on fire—ablaze with a grandly romantic and inextinguishable love for words.

You see, I understood quite early on that people tend to be products of their environments, their cultures and their heritage. As angry or frustrated as I might have gotten with someone, especially my father, I have long understood that if you accept where they're coming from, if you acknowledge that they can't help it, just as much we can't help feeling strongly about something ourselves—you enable yourself to let go of the negative emotions that tend to get you in trouble and waste so much precious time.

Thus, while I did not see my father as often as I might have liked as a child, I came to understand over time that my father always worked extraordinarily hard, in turn, giving my siblings and me extra ordinary opportunities by which to grow, appreciate and take advantage of this wonderful life.

Occasionally, whenever he drank too much and got emotional, my father would tell me a story about how his mother had slaved away and saved because she wanted her son to go to a special school across the border of Mexico in El Paso, Texas. Yet, my father refused to go because not only was he ashamed of their poverty, but felt guilty because they couldn't afford to buy him socks, let alone pay for his education. Thus, he only made it through the sixth grade.

At the age of nineteen, however, he decided to be the first of eight siblings to leave home and strike out on his own. He came to San Jose, California where he met my mother and a year later they married. A year after that I was born. We lived in a few different apartments my first few years and then in second grade, when I was six, we moved to a house on McEvoy Street with my two-year old sister and a newborn brother.

It was here that I think my life changed in the most positive way forever. It was here that I began a rather rich childhood, where the freedom of being the oldest child, left alone to explore and entertain himself, endowed me with so many experiences that I cherish in recollection. It is here where I learned about good and evil, about girls and boys, about pain and utter bliss. It is here where a fortunate childhood enabled me to envision all the possibilities of my life looking forward.

It is here where I learned to ride my bike, where Mary gave me my first kiss under the shade of a big tree, where I rolled in the mud with my two older cousins in the backyard, where in the giant empty lot next door, my friend Marcos and I experimentally smoked cigarettes pilfered from my Uncle Samuel—until we got caught and I had to apologize to him; it was one of the most embarrassing moments of my childhood, a moment that moved me to never smoke again.

105

The McEvoy house was also where I experienced, at the age of seven, my first peek at a naked adolescent girl, and subsequently the first stab of my libido that I can recall—it so happened that I got caught at that, too, when my father walked into the bedroom while I was peeking in the keyhole at my teenage cousin who had just stepped out of the shower.

Apart from all these fond and formative experiences of the earliest part of my carefree youth, McEvoy was also where my father started his furniture business in the basement of the house with his brother.

After toiling everyday at the old General Motors automotive plant in Fremont as a line assemblyman, my father would come home to work on upholstery jobs until late at night. Within a year or so, he had moved his burgeoning business down the street into a huge building where he built a manufacturing plant and a furniture retail store.

At the age of seven, I began to work for my father — on weekends, during summers and on holidays—sweeping the factory floor of all the sawdust and material scraps, making buttons for hours on end, and eventually making the furniture as well.

When I started, I earned fifty cents an hour and a pair of calloused hands. Although I was often exhausted and yearned to be out playing with the other children, I got to buy a lot of comic books. In retrospect, although these are not the fondest memories of my youth, I gained a vital work ethic that I applied fastidiously at school, to work, and to my greatest passions.

I also learned why hard work was so important to my father, for it not only provided him and his immediate family with the material wealth and comfort he never had growing up in Mexico, but it also afforded his children the opportunity to have an education like he never had.

But there was something even more necessary than diligence and perseverance in order to achieve success — he could envision all the possibilities.

That said, at a certain point there seemed to him a limit as to how far education could get you. He believed that a man had to begin working in order to earn a living and earn riches that might endow a life not bound by the limits of poverty.

Thus, he and I fought bitterly when I decided to go to graduate school. This frustrated both of us immensely, for he could not see the use of more school, and I could not convince him that I would be a fool not to continue increasing my earning potential. Thus, this time it was my turn to envision the possibilities.

In the end, I decided that, with or without his blessing and support, I was going back to school. After having spent four years at UCLA studying about all the wonders of the world through their international cultural studies program, I could not accept that the reward for all my academic adventures was a life of office work.

I began to envision and investigate the possibilities that would propel me beyond this disheartening mediocrity. I soon concluded that going back to school would be the most prudent choice.

And so, while working full-time as a cashier in the basement at the Fairmont Hotel at night, I also enrolled in the Masters program in Political Science at San Jose State University up the street.

After a semester I earned a few scholarships, bought my first Mac computer and got myself a job as a tutor in the university writing lab. Besides giving me the chance to focus on my studies, it also gave me the after-class and after-work resources where I wrote my first book at the age of 24. Although I never published it, I felt it was one of my first major accomplishments, giving me the confidence to keep on honing my writing skills for decades to come.

Eventually, I transferred from SJSU to the Masters of International and Public Affairs program at Columbia University. Once again, my father was emphatically against my decision and was particularly unhappy about my moving across the country to go to school again. Or at least that is how I initially perceived it.

Despite his opposition though, and with a nice gift from my mother, student loans, and a work-scholarship, I moved to New York in September of 1992.

After a semester at school, I started working as an events coordinator at the Latin American and Iberian Institute and became friends with one of the professors who had her office there.

One night, for whatever reason, I told her about my father's opposition to the furthering of my education. Her reply cast my father in a wholly different light for me. She said, "It's not that your father is against your education, he just didn't want you to leave the family, he didn't want you to move away." Her words struck at the center of me, because for whatever reason, I knew she was right.

> "I'm shakin' the dust of this crummy little town off my feet and I'm gonna see the world. Italy, Greece, the Parthenon, the Coliseum. Then, I'm comin' back here to go to college and see what they know. And then I'm gonna build things. I'm gonna build airfields, I'm gonna build skyscrapers a hundred stories high, I'm gonna build bridges a mile long..."
> **George Bailey, *It's a Wonderful Life***

Much like George Bailey in Frank Capra's classic film, It's a Wonderful Life, I had fantastically ambiguous big plans, just as I was ready to begin my life as an independent adult. Just like George, however, money matters inevitably took precedence over these lofty plans.

Back when I had just graduated from college and it came time to get a job, I begrudgingly acquiesced to my father's argument that writing, or anything art-related for that matter, was impractical. "How are you going to make any money doing that son?" he would say. Despite my chagrin, I knew he was right, for my dreams didn't involve any resolve to roll in the dough, get paid, to make money.

At the time, I was quite inexperienced and had little understanding about how money makes the world go around. I was also ignorant of the fact that as we begin to accumulate obligations and aspirations, we also accrue a need for more money to pay for them all.

Moreover, I had no notion whatsoever of the financial commitment involved in being a partner, a parent and a home owner—all of which costs a substantial sum of money, especially as you are increasingly pressured into keeping up with the neighbors.

108

Despite my dreams, I compromised, and for fifteen years now I have pursued a career in marketing, communications, and event development. I have not been able to apply my creative spirit and skills as freely and as often as I would have liked, but the work occasionally calls upon my creativity, and so it has kept me fairly happy. Moreover, I have had a fair share of success in the field, at least enough that financially I've been able to meet the demands of growing up and growing older.

Yet despite this success, I still neglected something that was much more important to me, because for most of my life I have repressed the urge to be a writer and an artist in earnest, and I've done what I thought was most practical and expected of me.

Instead of living *la vida loca*, I've traveled steadily along the straight and narrow: being studious and assiduous; finishing high school, college and then graduate school; getting a job; getting married, having kids, buying a home; and then getting a conservative and well-compensated corporate job, so that I could pay for all the things and obligations I had accumulated along the way; all the things that led me to this place, within these three carpeted grey walls, where I have spent 10-12 hours a day for the last seven years.

If you discount the personal and company holidays, that's approximately 2,300 hours a year that I spend paper pushing; add 2 hours of commuting a day to that, and you've got 2,760 hours committed to work alone—every year for the rest of my working life. If I'm lucky enough to retire at 65, with only 26 more years to go, that's a mere 71,760 hours more of cube time.

Guess it's no surprise that, for a while now, I've felt stuck inside this narrow tunnel of destiny; it was hard for me to envision anything outside my most immediate needs, my father's words haunting me: *make more money.*

But then, along came the digital revolution.
For the last four years or so I have toyed with digital video, stills, and design programs, creating many family photo albums and hundreds of illustrations to complement my tomes of verse.

I became fairly familiar with what digital could do, and I was happy to play with it, tinker and toy with it, experiment and explore all the possibilities that pixels, bits and bytes had to offer.

My true reversal of fortune, however, came with my separation and the sudden compulsion to employ my digital camera to fight off the ennui. Photography enabled me to utilize my technical skills, employ my aesthetic sensibility, and express my creativity in boundless ways. With the ease and versatility of digital equipment, along with amazing software and online services like flickr.com that support this medium, I began dreaming of artistic success more than ever before.

I began envisioning again.

Countless ideas arose while I was taking photos, and they poked at me mercilessly, moving me to work harder and more frantically than ever. At times, the feeling became quite overwhelming.

Be the change you wish to see in the world. **Gandhi**

Keep in mind that success is not determined by the past, but by what we see in the future. If we enable ourselves to see into the future by envisioning, by dreaming, by making-believe—we allow ourselves the possibility, and we move forward toward the first critical first step to success by thinking, "It just might happen!"

If you cannot envision what is possible above and beyond what already exists, you can't move forward, you can't progress, you can't build, you can't create, you can't innovate, and you surely can't be anything other than ordinary.

However, more important than being able to see into the future, is being able to envision the process that gets you there. It's this ability to strategically plan that makes all the difference.

For example, all great marketing considers and plans for three primary objectives:

> How do you get them to look? How do you get them to feel good about what they're looking at?
> And, how do you get them to desire what they feel good about, just enough so that they are willing to act upon this impulse or inspiration?

Thus, good marketing merely makes us look; great marketing makes us laugh and cry, and—*buy*.

Vision is the art of seeing the invisible.
Jonathan Swift

Before you take the next picture, remember to envision what the photo subject is going to look like within the greater context of its surroundings—What are the elements that are going to frame the subject that has caught your eye? What is at the periphery that may enhance or detract from your primary subject?

It is critical to be conscious of these peripheral factors, because as a whole they contribute and constitute the angle, depth, contrasts of form and color, lighting and iridescence (or complete lack thereof) of your picture. This is particularly true when you are photographing inanimate matter.

We don't see things as they are,
we see them as we are.
Anaïs Nin

By default, you should presume that your photo will look "flat," dully two-dimensional, especially if your subject is a still life.

Thus, it is incumbent upon you to bring your subject to life by taking a different tack than usual, get in closer, climb a tree, get on your belly, push outside your comfort zone and make an effort to extrapolate the extraordinary.

Much like my father envisioned a better life more than forty years ago and subsequently left his family in Mexico to start anew in sunny California, I too had to leave—going from sunny California to begin anew in the grand metropolis of New York City. For, I too had envisioned a better life for myself.

And, after coming full circle, after somehow ending up in the small-town suburbia that I had left ten years earlier, I once again knew it was time to look beyond, to envision a different life than the one I was leading, than the one that I felt was leading nowhere but into the DEAD END where small town dreamers go to die.

.

Lesson 24: Experiment

While I was living in the church, I challenged myself to go out to a different place in New York City every night, so I could take pictures. My adventures included trips to all five boroughs of New York City and many of the great neighborhoods and attractions in each including Astoria, Queens; across the Brooklyn Bridge to DUMBO; Coney Island at the tail end of Brooklyn; The Staten Island Ferry; and all throughout Manhattan—up and down all the Avenues, across all the streets, though Central Park, and gallivanting through hotspots like East and Greenwich Village, Chelsea and SoHo.

Pushing myself to get out and take pictures every night was an experiment of sorts for me. For, apart from the desire to keep busy, so that I would not sulk in the wake of my separation, I was vying to gain some intense and immediate experience and recognition as a photographer.

I feel this test was a success. For I felt that by being my own lab rat, I produced highly positive, if not extraordinary results.

Moreover and maybe more importantly, I ended up falling in love with the city all over again.

Ironically, my relationship with NYC evolved in a way that was quite akin to my marriage.

At first, I was bewitched, beguiled, and a sucker for every alluring twitch and turn. But then, when things got serious, and I had to work for a living, and I had to endure the mean streaks, the neuroses, the conniving, the paranoia and the general grumpy attitude of a lot of New Yorkers, I quickly became disenchanted.

After nearly a decade of being less than truly happy, however, circumstances radically changed for me, and in turn my appreciation and love for this City were renewed.

The place in particular that I fell in love with again was the Equator of Manhattan—42nd Street which has long been the vein that runs across the city, providing the pulse of the times. This zeitgeist-in-motion runs a little over two miles from the West Side Highway to the United Nations sitting on the East River.

Bordering this vibrant rue are some of the city's greatest landmarks including Port Authority, Times Square, Bryant Park, The Mid Manhattan Library, and of course, Grand Central Station.

With all the action constantly going on up and down 42nd Street, I found myself going back to this part of town often.

Times Square was a great place to experiment, because it was an extraordinary comb of energy, color and people from all walks of life—here, one could watch and run into and walk past everyone from waddling tourists, native New Yorkers hustling for a living on the street, pimps and prostitutes and police, hordes of teens trying to get a glimpse of starlight from below the MTV studios, the Bridge and Tunnel crowd—either clubbing or looking to catch a show on Broadway, and the many transient folks like me who were merely passing through on their way to work or home.

With all this hustle and bustle going on, there were countless opportunities to have fun with the camera, to challenge myself to get interesting photos, to experiment and take risks for the sake of growing as a photographer and creating the extraordinary as an artist.

It was here that I began taking a lot of photos with my camera sitting on the street or sidewalk. It was here that I walked through crowds and took random shots of strangers passing. It was here that I held my camera high above the masses of people around me and attempted to get photos from a bird's eye view. It was here that I stood smack in the middle of streets and captured pedestrians walking by like cosmopolitan spirits. It was here that I would literally circle groups of people and take pictures of them inconspicuously as they gawked at the towering billboards and thousands of lights that make this place a Mecca for people from all over the world. It was here that I really pushed myself to see the world in as many ways as possible in order to enlighten myself with all the possibilities.

It was here that I was reminded that I must constantly challenge myself and test my limits—as a photographer, as an artist, as a man, as a father, as a partner, as a social person, as an individual, but most of all, as a human being.

114

The great thing about experimenting with digital photography is that if something new doesn't work for you...well, all you have to do is trash the photos. Just a couple of clicks and you can forget about all the ghastly, blurry, really-really bad photos you took during your little experiment.

Either way, make sure you try to learn from such mistakes, so that you do not waste time making them again in the future.

New perspectives are often the most rewarding, because they allow you to renew the old and appreciate anew what is often overlooked or taken for granted by others.

So, venture out into the wild, go where you've never thought of going to photograph that same old street you tromp down every day on your way to work—climb to a rooftop, go down an alley, stop at a corner and watch others walk by.

Or simply hold your camera up high, place it down low—just find a new and exciting and bold way of seeing the world with this wonderful third eye of yours.

Lesson 25: Be Yourself

Many of the lessons in this book are fluid, they are not concrete; they are not pebbles that one can readily sort into piles of discrete wisdom. There is much crossover and overlap and undertow, to and fro, pulling and pushing, as well as interlocking-interlacing, and letting go.

In the end, though, I think all the wisdom you ever learn can be boiled down into one platitude, one saw, one ontological root, one proverbial summary of all we know:

Be Yourself

The irony here is, of course, that such simple wisdom sounds much like the standard Madison Avenue spiel—slick advertising slogans that actually aim to make you just like everyone else.

Thus, besieged by advertising everywhere, despite our greatest efforts, our aspirations to be an individual, sometimes only seem to get harder.

Nonetheless and allthemore, the goal remains the same. For being yourself not only means understanding what pleases you in this life, in the here and now, but it also means accepting your idiosyncrasies, and not being afraid of showing them off to others.

Moreover, being yourself means being yourself. In other words, it means actively pursuing those things that tickle you, that move you, that make your day.

It means following your bliss.

Individuals are ever evolving—as a result, we are often faced with the dilemma of choosing between satisfying our simple needs—and satisfying those needs of society, the community, and everyone else.

Sometimes something suits us quite well, and for a while it becomes who we are and who we project ourselves to be.

But occasionally, if not often, our circumstances and tastes change, so that the trademark gesture or outfit or manner of speech that identifies us as individuals no longer befits who we are becoming and care to be.

The problem becomes that others expect consistency. We are pressured to stick to precedent, to maintain what we ourselves may have fashioned into the status quo.

This is especially true when it concerns our values, beliefs, and commitments.

God forbid you change your mind!

But, alas, it happens all the time and we get stuck in the middle of the whirlwinds that pull us apart. And even if our alterations do not qualify as whimsy, we often still face the peril of "Why?"

Oh, how wonderful it would be if we could satisfactorily answer everyone with an earnest "Why not?" and get on with it—to move on, to enjoy whatever it is we have chosen or revived or contrived anew.

Perhaps, more difficult to contend with than the undulating inclinations themselves, is the application of what we would like to call our own, that which we have created alone and which distinguishes us by its rendering.

Sometimes, even the most innocuous things are bitterly contended or rallied against by others because they do not conform to the way "everyone else" perceives or believes or concedes that we should all uniformly behave. Sometimes it is as frivolous as fashion, a small personal touch that raises eyebrows and spurs some to knee-jerk in response, "You know, that's not how you wear it…"

Stick to your guns. Be true to yourself and act upon what makes you happy. People will either come to accept your so-called quirks and idiosyncrasies or just write you off as an eccentric.

After three months of virtual isolation at the Little Church, I moved back home in an attempt to abet the reconciliation that we had been fostering during our separation.

Ultimately, things really did not improve, as hard as we tried. By the end of 2005 we were virtually separated again, but simply living in the same house. To avoid the arguments that had started up again, I stayed out of the house as much as possible, often staying late at work to work on my budding passion of photography.

However, my art could only sustain me for so long. Once again, I began feeling as if I were on the precipice of a meltdown. I was solemn a little too often and was becoming desperate for a change.

One day on my way to work I came to the conclusion that beyond the bad marriage, perhaps I was going through my third mid-life crises. The first was when I turned 30, the second came around 35, and now, ever closer to the sharp edge of 40, I was feeling the pressure of realizing meaning—of being able to readily answer the question of what have I done with my life to make it worthy, of being able to smile and affirmatively answer that I have indeed made the right choices and that I am leading the life that I deeply desire to lead.

The unusually overwhelming feeling I began having in the fall and through winter was—"I want more."

Usually, I'm the guy encouraging others to be happy with what they have, and certainly I do have a lot—my family that loves me and that I love immensely, and of course there is that handful of friends that I have maintained through the years; a great job; a house, a home, a passion for life, an über-awareness of my surroundings, a generously giving and supportive wife; so what more could I want from life?

Yet despite all that, I readily recognized and tendered, that I was still feeling that I should be surrendering to something else, that I should be following a different bliss

One night in January of 2006, I went out to see a movie, *Brokeback Mountain.* I was particularly moved by the story of the pursuit of the character's passion despite all the odds; despite all the risks, and all the harmful thoughts and actions of others.

When I came home that evening I asked my wife for the final separation with the ultimate intention of divorce. I just couldn't compromise life anymore, I wanted to pursue life as I saw fit without having to often compromise my happiness, my passions, and the spirit of my life. I was confident that somehow we would work things out with the children; I was certain that the boys would not be downtrodden by the divorce, but rather would benefit in the midst of the serenity gained via their parents' separate lives.

Moreover, I was ecstatic by the idea that I might now have the opportunity to teach them by example. That if I followed my bliss, that I pursued my passions for writing and photography and made something of these talents that I would ultimately accomplish something extraordinary as an individual, and that this alone would be a great lesson to teach my children.

Thus, eventually I moved out again five months after my declaration. In the interim, I worked diligently at my arts and began gaining much greater recognition than I could ever imagine. By April of 2007 over 200 blogs had featured over 350 of my photographs; by the end of May there were 225 and 375 respectively . Moreover, many of my photos have been selected for special features on online magazines, and FOTO*Magazin,* Germany's premier photography magazine printed an article on my cut-out technique in their July 2006 issue.

On May 1st, 2006 I finally moved back out and into Manhattan to the very same apartment I lived in over a decade ago.

And it is practically the very same apartment I lived in ten years ago. People still stay up till the wee hours of the morning yelling and screaming and hollering on the street. Drug dealers still sit on my stoop and peddle and push and run whenever the lookout sees an officer coming around the corner. Babies are still having babies; the little girls that ran up and down this five-floor walk-up when I first lived there, now are little women who sit on the stoop with a cell phone in one hand and a baby stroller in the other.

Fortunately, at the time of my second separation, my dear friend Robert was still living in the apartment. I moved in in 1993, he moved in a year later; and only until now, did he decide to move out to live with his new bride. It was a strangely beautiful coincidence.

Or was it? Because at the same time that I was on the brink of making the ultimate decision, our friend Rayner was also going through his separation. Rayner also has two young children. Rayner also had been married for eight years. Rayner also lived in this very same apartment almost ten years ago. We lived there, together, only for a week, but we became best of friends nonetheless (and allthemore). For while I was moving out to go live with my new bride in a brownstone in Brooklyn, he was moving in with his girlfriend, soon to be wife.

Hence, here we both were, *The Odd Couple Anew*, at the beginning of summer, in oddly similar situations, both needing a place to stay, both needing to find a way to transition back to where we once were before.

It so happened that Robert's other roommate was moving out as well. Thus, a month apart, Rayner and I moved back into the very same apartment we lived in ten years ago.

They say life is one big circle—I'm beginning to believe it is all too true.

And so I moved in. I took the smallest of the three bedrooms, a 10 x 8 foot box—big enough for a bed, a desk and my beloved books. Wind regularly blew in soot from the surrounding metropolis to cover the counters and line all the window sills until a fine gray layer told me it was time to wipe them clean. Cracks decorated the off-white walls with random streaks pouring down the buckling plaster.

Still, I was okay with this. As a consequence of my decision, the material comforts and the convenience of having everything in one place is now a luxury I can longer afford. However, as I had done once before, I adapted, and I learned to live with a lot less.

Still, I'll admit, for a while, in the beginning I wasn't always okay with this. When old friends visited and commented that my new home felt like a college dormitory or they looked at me annoyed and incredulously when I said that I couldn't afford to go out with them to a moderately priced Manhattan restaurant— it hurt. And although I knew I had a lot more than most—a roof, a warm bed, enough to eat, a strong will, maybe, some creative talent—still I couldn't help but feel somewhat impoverished somehow.

And still, what really ached and ailed me more than anything was each and every time I had to bid farewell to the boys. After I kissed and hugged them tightly, and said goodnight with the biggest smile I could muster—I had to turn and run away to the bus stop as soon as possible, so that they didn't see the pain that I was feeling inside, so that they didn't see the tears that threatened my manhood, because this is simply something I just couldn't hide, once I'd said—"Goodbye."

Even though I tried, I wasn't exactly feeling as if the apartment was much of a "home."

To console myself I often thought, "Perhaps, than, as I have long yearned to make true, the world is really my home." Because oddly enough, I had come to feel over the last year that I was actually quite at home when I'm taking pictures, which was often alone on the grimy and gritty streets of New York City.

In essence, after a few months of getting used to the new arrangement, getting used to once again not seeing the boys everyday, and getting used to the lack of creature comforts of home, I began to truly feel it had been the right choice because I genuinely felt that I was regaining a sense of self, a sense of who I truly was and wanted to become in life.

Moreover, I was feeling happier than ever as I pursued my bliss—writing like mad to make up for lost time and continuing to take thousands of photos of the street life of New York City.

We are all on a quest. We all are seeking ourselves when we live life and find ourselves asking what does it all mean? The answer lies in learning to accept and nurture your individuality, learning to *be yourself.*

Acknowledgements

I would like to thank all those who made this book possible via their tolerance, love and support.

First and foremost, I would like to profusely thank my editor for the book, Stephanie Staal, without whom this book would have never have been written. She believed in me and my work and for that I will be forever grateful. It is no surprise that she has subsequently become one of my best friends and confidants over the last two years.

I would also like to thank my boys, Enzo and Nicky for being such tolerant photography subjects and for often inspiring me to be myself more than ever. Thanks also goes to my ex, Domenica, especially for being such a great mother to our children; my parents, Mom and Pops; and my siblings, Sabina and Daniel.

I am also quite grateful to my in-laws, Nancy and John; as well as my sister-in-laws, and their husbands, for all the emotional and logistical support given after I left home.

Just as importantly, I would like to thank all those great friends, who have supported me (and my writing in particular) through their encouragement, inspiration and amity over the years: Claudio Kaufmann, Feyza Marouf, Marie Huber, Mia Schleifer, Rayner Ramirez, Rebecca Evans, Robert Thomas, Sandrine Tesner, Shana Franklin, Sola O'Connell, and Suzanne Hogan.

A special thank you goes to Chelsea Hollander and Gillian Leigh for both their friendship and the great photos they took of me for the HP Be Brilliant advertising campaign.

I would also like to thank all the aspiring photographers from around the world who sent me letters over the last couple of years attesting to how inspirational my words and photos have been for them; especially since their words and photos have been just as inspirational to me.

Finally, I would like to thank all the writers and wise men (and women) who have inspired me throughout my life. I tried to share a few of their words with this book; I hope that you, the reader, have likewise felt inspired by them.

May your life be rife with intrigue, joy and adventure. *Lorenzo*

About The Author

Lorenzo is an author, a writer and an award-winning street photographer.

He has written numerous books, interviews and articles about fine art and photography for En Foco, *Nueva Luz,* Rain Tiger and the Examiner.

Throughout most of 2010, his book, *25 Lessons I've Learned about ~~photography~~ Life!* has been the #1 Best Selling Photo Essay and Artist & Photography Biography on Amazon.com. Paul Giguere, guru for the popular podcast thoughts on photography, considers *25 Lessons* one of the "classic" essays on photography.

In October of 2010, he served as the NYC photography adviser for the recently launched Microsoft foursquare photography app. In 2008, he was chosen to be the HP Be Brilliant Featured Artist.

Since taking up digital photography in 2005, his photography has been featured in *fotoMAGAZIN,* Germany's premier photo magazine, and his photos have been cited, posted and published by over 350 other blogs, websites, and print publications.

Today, Lorenzo has over 32,000 photographs published on flickr.com—one of the world's most popular photography websites—where his photos have been seen over 6 million times and where he ranks as one of the site's most popular photographers (aka "lorenzodom").

He has been called an "Internet photography sensation" by *Time Out New York* and is considered a "Flickr star" by Rob Walker, Consumed columnist, for *New York Times Magazine.*

His work is represented worldwide by Getty Images.

Praise for 25 Lessons

The Catcher in the Rye generation now has a new book to call their favorite, finally!

Forget learning about being in the power of now—forget reading about stopping to appreciate life—forget studying how to see the special moments—this book is the experience, it is the moment.

After reading 25 Lessons you can no longer settle for your status quo. Lorenzo! steals the night, capturing all he sees, teaching us through photography what he experiences as he goes through a metamorphosis from the inside out.

If you yourself don't drastically change after reading, aren't purely inspired, then start on page one again, because you weren't listening. Take it all in and begin on your own journey of self-discovery.

Beth Jannery, Author of *Simple Grace:*
Living a Meaningful Life

"...I had never seen any other photographer who was able to capture the essence of NYC street life in such a unique and distinctive style... in many of my conversations on great photographers, I frequently mention Lorenzo's work and prided myself for my early stage recognition of his talent.

Lorenzo has been able to capture moments in time, which allow the viewer to study relationships that cannot be observed in the real-time dynamics of life. Even more intriguing are Lorenzo's sequential photographs, each one remarkable in itself, but viewed together are nothing less that a visual urban poem. It has been my pleasure to watch Lorenzo's rapid growth as a leading photographer of our time."
Jim Van Meter : Rochester, NY, USA

"... No hace falta entender de fotografía ni ser un experto en temas formales de técnica, luz o composición para quedarte sin palabras delante de su obra. Y eso, probablemente, es lo mejor.

Sus fotografías llegan a todo el mundo, independientemente de la edad, religión, nacionalidad o estatus social.

Lorenzo adora Nueva York y eso se nota. Retrata como nadie su ciudad, sus gentes, sus colores, sus sentimientos y, en general, su atmósfera. En realidad, todo se resume en la esencia; como fotógrafo, no reproduce simplemente lo que tiene delante, sino que es capaz de capturar su esencia, su espíritu. Y eso, que él consigue en cada foto de manera natural, es algo realmente muy difícil de alcanzar."
Carmen Padró: Barcelona, Spain

"Lorenzo é um grande fotógrafo, entrar em seu flickr é a certeza de poesia em forma de fotos, um raro talento, habilidade excepcional em se comunicar através das imagens. Sua fotografia é movimento, emoção, um olhar atento, apurado e artístico do mundo que nos cerca, por onde transitam cores, formas, impressões e muita paixão. É um prazer ímpar poder admirar sua obra e seu belíssimo trabalho..."
Leni Miranda: Rio de Janeiro, Brasil

"Let's cut to the chase: Lorenzo is a master. His body of work is some of the very best on flickr and may very well be some of the best being done in the medium today. His street/city work follows in the tradition of Paul Strand, Cartier-Bresson, Garry Winogrand and Larry Friedlander. But he doesn't simply imitate nor work within previously defined boundaries. Lorenzo's "street" approach goes beyond studied and safe, offering new vision, compelling the viewer to see what they have seen before differently... freshly. Lorenzo's work is not limited to a single genre. He transcends categorization…Great, great stuff. Inspired and inspiring... and educational.
Lorenzo's 25 Lessons are a must for anyone who raises a camera to their eye. They are well thought out, deceptively simple—easy to grasp—and applicable to all phases of the photographic art, as seminal a piece of writing on the how of photography as Ansel's dissertation on the zone system. And make no mistake, they are not (merely) a basic primer for

beginners. I found them to be reenergizing, perceptive and extremely useful.

No one can create images as Lorenzo has without integrating the tenets of discerning vision and the richness of details of life without having an extraordinary level of passion. It is clear Lorenzo is passionate—about his work... and about life. I have been touched by his story, his writings and by his work. I can't imagine anyone not being so."
Barry Shapiro: Los Angeles, CA, USA

"Literary and photographic genius. A man of the people. A fraction of what half of us could only wish to be. Keep up the inspiration Lorenzo."
John Terry: Newcastle, UK

"Lorenzo...has a passion for life, photography and writing. He is a linguistic genius, a storyteller through words and pictures. He captures with his camera the world as he sees it, its feelings, love, beauty and all it that it has to offer..."
Brenda George: Adelaide, Australia

"This guy is amazing...Many photos are shot with an old Canon PowerShot—how many people are able to get out the best of this rather vintage camera? The themes, angles and exposure are brilliant!"
Christoph Moser: Germany

Photographer Lorenzo Dominguez has the uncanny ability to find beauty in his surroundings. Also gifted in the use of words, his book, 25 Lessons, is much more than the typical tech manual on photography. It's more like a roadmap for using your heart, soul and senses to capture images through the lens of a camera.

When a change in life events had him soul searching, Lorenzo took to the streets of New York with his camera, photographing every night using his digital "point-and-shoot" cameras. He was mesmerized by the color and movement of the city and feels that "pictures see what we do not see." His mantra is that the craft is liberating and everything possesses its own beauty. He stresses the allure of black and white images because they emphasize form. Inspired by paintings of the masters, they train his eye for the use of color in photos.

25 Lessons rekindles passion in photographers and photojournalists. Reading Lorenzo's advice can spark and stir the Muse to grand proportions. He offers strong advice to always have your camera ready to shoot. He also advises shutterbugs to employ their imagination and see the world with child-like eyes. One main ingredient he specifically looks for in his subjects is attitude. This is apparent in many of his photos. The choice of backgrounds is as important as the people in them. Read his book and you will fall in love not only with photography but also in the area in which you live, regardless of its socioeconomic standing.

Serving as a mentor, Lorenzo covers the importance of persevering, staying calm and seizing the moment. Any successful person can confirm this. His eye for the unusual, results in extraordinary shots worthy of emulation. From contrast to optical illusion, he inspires others to lighten up and think outside of the box.

Photographing the Big Apple, a city with "aesthetic milk and honey," he found that it offered him endless wells of inspiration. An honest and often candid view of life is what he peddles on flickr, a photo sharing site, and elsewhere. His desire is to help others do the same. He challenges fellow photographers to "make something out of nothing." It's a thought that sounds Seinfeld-like in sentiment. Perhaps there's a kinship with the show about nothing; he likewise emphasizes the importance of employing humor in the craft.

25 Lessons will fire you up to dust off your camera and hit the street running. You will gain a fresh perspective on seeing things you've never noticed before or previously took for granted. Not only is his book valuable for writers and photographers, but anyone who needs a fresh outlook on life.

Phyllis Johnson, photojournalist and author of *Being Frank with Anne* & *Hot and Bothered By It*. Virginia, USA

Anyone who has been treated to Lorenzo's writing knows what a creative shakeup ensues in the reader. 25 Lessons combines Lorenzo's unique gift for verbal expression with the eye of a lover and ever-discoverer of New York City, arguably the best beat a photographer can cast his eyes upon. Lorenzo's writing is an invitation to the creator in each of us: poetic and gritty like the city it describes, exotic at times, explosive when warranted, and always original, it titillates the imagination, re-energizes the lost soul, and fuels a desire for emulation. Between the pen and the lens, Lorenzo has paid a great homage to a city which more than any other embodies LIFE in all its vibrant and surprising dimensions.

Sandrine Tesner: Paris, France

As an oncologist, my primary job is not only to add days to people's lives, it is to add life to people's days. Lorenzo's book has provided me with a great instrument through which I can further become the counselor, healer and confidant my patient's demand. It has reignited in me the passion, warmth and compassion which are sequential for me on a daily basis to be the best physician and person I can be and I've encouraged all of my patients and families to share in his masterpiece as laughter, love, and imagination are the ultimate weapons against grief and despair. Secondary to Lorenzo's great influence in my life, I continue to use his writings and photography as a means to inspire my patient's to express their deep inner emotions as a way to reflect on their understanding of disease and in developing goals of therapy. I recommend his book to all.
Mike Rotkowitz, MD: New York City

While this would be plenty interesting if it were only about photography, 25 Lessons is about so much more. Lorenzo's journey and experiences are truly inspiring, and the photographs really capture the essence of life in New York--a real feat. This book is full of love, faith, hope, and courage. Perfect for passing on to friends.

Christina

Other Books by Lorenzo

A Letter to A Muse

A Letter to A Muse is a collection of poetry which was written almost entirely in the Fall of 2002, as a letter of introduction to poet and writer I hold in high esteem.

There are 222 illustrated poems in this volume. Half are originals created solely by the author. The vast majority were written between August and December of 2002.

The subsequent half of the book consists of entries inspired by other poet's celebrated work. Some are purposeful parodies, others playful parities—all serious inquisition and introspection. The vast majority of these poems were written in response to the reading of the other poem, and a scant few simply thematically matched previously written work.

In addition to the 222 poems that make up the original concept of the book, there are also 27 other extra poems that have never been made public before.

Art Matters

Chronicles of Love, Lust and Debauchery Selected Prose and Verse, 2005-2008

Art Matters, it really does.

It drives my life, and gives it meaning; much as my amazing family and friends, and the adventures I have with them, often do.

Art Matters is a compendium of three years of work from the summer of 2005 until the beginning of summer 2008.

There are over 400 pages here of over 200 entries, with just as many photos and images to complement the prose and verse.

Art Matters is as much introspective and idiosyncratic, as it strives to induce the laws of human nature and the universe.

It is also honest, for I have long believed that to be a great artist you cannot fear what others might think of you and the genuine life you dare lead. A great artist must present the truth

as only she sees and feels it. Otherwise, she will fail miserably at
the task.

Be Yourself

A celebration of the spirit of the individual as captured on the
streets of New York City
100 photographs of individuals on the streets and subways of
New York City. Each photograph is complemented by a quote
about individuality, genius or self-determination.

the lost man chronicles
book 1, the art of living

Written in a manner akin to the parables of Jesus Christ and
the free flowing prose of Elbert Herbert's White Hyacinths, the
lost man chronicles relays a depth of understanding similar to
that conveyed by the likes of Lao-tse, the Bhagavad-Gita, Plato,
and Nietzsche.

The lost man chronicles is a modern day testament to one
man's journey to become re-immersed in a world which has been
lost in the glare of modern convenience and commercial
contrivances. Each passage explores a passage toward
enlightenment, toward awareness, and ultimately toward
rediscovering the meaning of life.
Simple to read and easy to understand, the lost man chronicles is
accessible to all. Yet, as facile each passage is to comprehend, as
a whole, the work is bound to have profound impact on those
who read it.

Entry 1 (of 100)

losing thy self

i am a man who has lost his self. one no longer another amongst all the others, but an entity which is one with the world.

amalgamated into this universal wonder i am apt to wander through like a molecule brushing up against others, floating, swirling, lingering when i am cold, frantic when i am not.

sometimes, from a distance, i may seem indistinguishable, but look a little closer and, and you'll discover i'm unique.

in my purest form i am energy. but when i use my self through mortal toil i am apt to waste both time and space, to channel my self through and towards no means necessary, to err merely for the sake of escaping ennui.

this is why i have lost my self. because i want to know me, i want to know purity, the untainted possibilities of being nothing, yet everything, again.

"the less there is of you, the more you experience the sublime."
Joseph Campbell

StreetWise: How to be a Great Photographer, Lessons Learned on the Streets of New York City

The 25 Lessons Trilogy: 25 Lessons I've Learned (about photography); 25 More Lessons (I've Learned); and 25 Points of Creativity

StreetWise, How to be a Great Photographer, Lessons Learned on the Streets of New York City, was written by the bestselling author of 25 Lessons I've Learned about Photography, and is comprised of the original 25 Lessons I've Learned (about Photography) that served as the primary inspiration for the book. (http://www.25lessons.com).

In addition, included are also the sequels, 25 More Lessons (I've Learned) and 25 Points of Creativity, to complete the 25 Lessons Trilogy.

This is a must for any aspiring artist or creative spirit, whether you're a photographer, writer, painter or advertising agency creative director this volume of wisdom will inspire you page after page after page.

Each lesson is illustrated with pertinent images, many of the photographs taken by Lorenzo when he wrote these treatises on creativity when living in a small church in the middle of Manhattan in the Spring of 2005.

10997829R0

Made in the USA
Lexington, KY
02 September 2011